MUSCLE CARS

IN DETAIL   No. 11

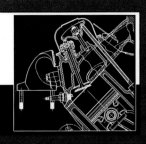

1970
Plymouth SUPERBIRD

ROAD RUNNER SUPERBIRD

Plymouth

IT'S A RARE BIRD

Geoff Stunkard

CarTech®

CarTech®

CarTech®, Inc.
838 Lake Street South
Forest Lake, MN 55025
Phone: 651-277-1200 or 800-551-4754
Fax: 651-277-1203
www.cartechbooks.com

© 2018 by Geoff Stunkard

All rights reserved. No part of this publication may be reproduced or utilized in any form or by any means, electronic or mechanical, including photocopying, recording, or by any information storage and retrieval system, without prior permission from the Publisher. All text, photographs, and artwork are the property of the Author unless otherwise noted or credited.

The information in this work is true and complete to the best of our knowledge. However, all information is presented without any guarantee on the part of the Author or Publisher, who also disclaim any liability incurred in connection with the use of the information and any implied warranties of merchantability or fitness for a particular purpose. Readers are responsible for taking suitable and appropriate safety measures when performing any of the operations or activities described in this work.

All trademarks, trade names, model names and numbers, and other product designations referred to herein are the property of their respective owners and are used solely for identification purposes. This work is a publication of CarTech, Inc., and has not been licensed, approved, sponsored, or endorsed by any other person or entity. The Publisher is not associated with any product, service, or vendor mentioned in this book, and does not endorse the products or services of any vendor mentioned in this book.

Edit by Wes Eisenschenk
Layout by Monica Seiberlich

ISBN 978-1-61325-300-7
Item No. CT578

Library of Congress Cataloging-in-Publication Data

Names: Stunkard, Geoff (Geoffrey F.), author.
Title: 1970 Plymouth Superbird : in detail / Geoff Stunkard.
Description: Forest Lake, MN : CarTech, [2018]
Identifiers: LCCN 2017034659 | ISBN 9781613253007
Subjects: LCSH: Plymouth automobile. | Plymouth automobile--History. | Automobiles--United States--History.
Classification: LCC TL215.P65 S88 2018 | DDC 629.222/2--dc23
LC record available at https://lccn.loc.gov/2017034659

Written, edited, and designed in the U.S.A.
Printed in China
10 9 8 7 6 5 4 3 2 1

Front Cover:
John Balow of Muscle Car Restorations restored this FY1 yellow Superbird, which was seen during the reconstruction of Bristol Motor Speedway. It was formerly a pace car at a short track and is powered by the 440 U-code engine.

Frontispiece:
The reason the cars were built was to get this driver, Richard Petty, back into a Plymouth. Seen here at the fall race in Talladega, King Richard would have certainly won the World Championship save for a devastating and race-missing accident at Darlington in mid-season. (Ray Mann Photo, Courtesy Cal Lane)

Title Page:
The 1970 Plymouth Superbird was considered the most flamboyant Road Runner of them all when the dust finally settled on the model's tenure in 1980. (Steve Netkow Photo)

Table of Contents:
A group of Superbirds and Charger Daytonas roll down to the front stretch. They returned to the storied banking of Talladega in 2015 for a special reunion, one of a number of events that focus on these unique cars.

DISTRIBUTION BY:
Europe
PGUK
63 Hatton Garden
London EC1N 8LE, England
Phone: 020 7061 1980 • Fax: 020 7242 3725
www.pguk.co.uk

Australia
Renniks Publications Ltd.
3/37-39 Green Street
Banksmeadow, NSW 2109, Australia
Phone: 2 9695 7055 • Fax: 2 9695 7355
www.renniks.com

Canada
Login Canada
300 Saulteaux Crescent
Winnipeg, MB, R3J 3T2 Canada
Phone: 800 665 1148 • Fax: 800 665 0103
www.lb.ca

TABLE OF CONTENTS

629. 222 Dr

DEDICATION

To the unsung heroes of car collecting, both known and unknown, who solidified the Superbird and sister Charger Daytona as truly unique icons of both OEM production and the glory days of the Grand National series early on. Your efforts are both recognized and rewarded by those who have followed.

ACKNOWLEDGMENTS

Honestly, this was a trying book project for me, as much of my previous work has been focused more on narrative than technical process. To that end, my sincerest thanks goes out to expert Frank Badalson, who gave unselfishly of his time, resources, and energy in this project; any mistakes are mine, not his. To Tony D'Agostino for similar reference help, and a 120-mph wing car ride on circa-1970 Polyglas tires when we were young and foolish. Once in a lifetime, pal!

To racing collectors Doug Schellinger, Tim Wellborn, and Todd Werner, for access to wonderful vehicles with real race history as well as associated paperwork. To groundbreaking wing car author, Frank Moriarty for permission to use his previous interviews in this project. To historian, David Patik, who also supplied editorial suggestions and invaluable OEM reference material on Lynch Road. To Jeff Wickstrom on the unwinged 'Bird story, and Sue George for her referral to Jeff. To Galen Aasland for the land-speed information.

To car owners, many unnamed but including Smith Stokes, Greg and Kathleen Mosley, John Balow, Dale Mathews, Don Fezell, Ryan Clough, and Dale Keuhn among others. Don Garlits and Steve Reyes secured use of and photography on the Burnt Orange 'Bird from the Garlits Museum; thank you.

Once again, Calvin Lane gets credit for access to Ray Mann's amazing NASCAR images, with other photos coming from Tom McCrea, Mike Hill, and Galen Aasland, and continued gratitude to Brandt Rosenbusch for materials from FCAs files. To Galen Govier for his extensive numeric research on parts and dating. To Wes Eisenschenk for dealing with me when I got up on the tires and headed for the wall as well as excellent ad research. Likewise, to my wife Linda for the same patience. Isaiah 40:31 says, "But those who hope in the Lord will renew their strength. They will soar on wings like eagles; they will run and not grow weary; they will walk and not be faint."

For one great season, it was fun while it lasted.

INTRODUCTION

The era covered in the following pages is unique in automotive history. The power of "Win on Sunday, Sell on Monday" marketing actually came to its peak moment just as the Plymouth Superbird arrived on the scene. Ford, General Motors, and Chrysler started the 1970 model year with very aggressive performance car marketing; this special vehicle was one of many that came out in the 1969–1970 model era to homologate, or legalize, components for racing. To the companies involved, victory was worth that much.

By the end of that year, however, there had been wholesale changes as Detroit began focusing all energies on urgent and upcoming government regulations. The Superbird, built on a tight schedule in limited numbers, not only fell from grace in the OEM environment but also on the very racetracks it had been created for, as NASCAR made radical rules changes in 1971 to basically eliminate these special packages. Perhaps looked upon oddly as street cars when first released, ownership of one of these vehicles became a goal of the earliest efforts at collecting muscle cars a mere decade later.

A parallel movement by fans of NASCAR started with gatherings and clubs specifically for these unique aerocars, and by the 21st Century, their values had become well established, justifying expensive restorations and purchase prices. In this book, I recount some facts that have been recognized in prior tomes, as well as provide additional background on how the Superbird came to be, how it performed in its over-too-soon moment in competition, and its modern-day popularity. Come fly with us.

Collector Don Fezell's unrestored low-mileage U-code Superbird was part of his amazing racing and muscle car collection. It sold at Mecum's 2017 auction in Florida.

7

The former Walter P. Chrysler Museum near Detroit displays the Airflow models of the 1930s that were the forerunners to the aerodynamic stylings that arrived in the late 1960s for racing. (Photo Courtesy Quartermilestones.com)

Inasmuch as exercises in automotive styling were usually done by designers, it is fitting that something as outrageous as the Plymouth Superbird emerged from the engineering side of the Chrysler Corporation. After all, Walter P. Chrysler's own personal interest in how and why things worked had been part of the company's DNA since its 1924 founding. Moreover, the first scientific aero-restyling in the automotive realm was the Chrysler Airflow of the 1930s. The victim of being "too much too soon" in its overall innovations, the Airflow effort could conceivably be seen as the grandfather of what came to pass when the company threw away normalcy in the pursuit of scientific success years later, even though the latter occasion was based on a much narrower purpose: winning races.

THE POST-WAR BOOM AND THE TOWNSEND ERA

Following World War II, peacetime brought about a huge interest in motorsports. Participation grew exponentially in amateur and professional auto racing. Regardless of the form of the contest, after sheer horsepower accomplished all that was possible, engineers and racers began to think about aerodynamics. They quickly realized that there was something to it and that aerodynamics could take a competitor back to the front of the pack. Without fully realizing it, "Big Bill" France and his National Association for Stock Car Auto Racing (NASCAR) circuit likely played the biggest role in what turned Detroit's attention to aerodynamics in

The Superbird was similarly created as a testament to pure function, as restorer John Balow demonstrates at Bristol Motor Speedway. (Photo Courtesy Quartermilestones.com)

Owner Ray Nichels and driver Paul Goldsmith were hired by fellow Indy car luminary Ronney Householder, who had headed up Chrysler's racing efforts since the 1950s. Goldsmith put this Plymouth on the pole for the 1964 Daytona 500. (Ray Mann Photo, Courtesy Cal Lane)

production cars. France's monstrous new paved race course in Daytona Beach was a showcase of factory pride from its 1959 opening.

Soon after, Chrysler's board of directors selected a former outside auditor and then-current comptroller named Lynn Townsend to take the reins of the firm in July 1961. Although the company was in the red financially, Townsend recognized what it meant to see a car from Chrysler's stables show its prowess on the Daytona track. In October 1961, he authorized a new racing-focused group at Chrysler Engineering to develop competition packages for both NASCAR and drag racing.

That done, Chrysler's longtime racing liaison Ronney Householder went to Highland, Indiana, and hired his former Indy car associate Ray Nichels and driver Paul Goldsmith to help spearhead Chrysler's NASCAR development. Formerly with Pontiac, Nichels was a skilled fabricator and seasoned race team owner. He became the primary developer of engineered components for Chrysler's circle track program as well as its distributor to other teams.

As a brand, Plymouth already had one of the most noted names in the Grand National series. This name, of course, was Petty. Lee Petty posted season championships during the previous decade and also won the first big race at the new Daytona 500 track in 1959. Racing

in a full-size Plymouth, he was badly injured in a crash at the same Daytona event during qualifying in 1961. After his son Richard took over driving full-time, the team became Chrysler's primary full-time campaigner.

With Nichels and the factory responsible for development and the Petty crew (along with other campaigners) taking care of the week-in/week-out real-world testing, the work to win races as a corporation began in earnest. Chrysler had already moved to its unitized construction chassis design, eliminating the need for a heavy full frame. Meanwhile, engineers led by Tom Hoover, a Penn State–trained physicist who loved hot rodding as a hobby, had taken the RB-series Chrysler engine to its most functionally practical limits for racing. They laid plans to reintroduce the legendary Chrysler Hemi-design cylinder head to the roaring 1960s.

THE NEED FOR SPEED

Townsend wanted a winner for Daytona by 1964. Beginning in March 1963, Hoover and his crew set their sights on taking the first-generation Hemi cylinder head and adapting it to a revised extreme-duty RB engine block for that purpose. Working under a very tight schedule, these engines were hand-fitted and tested rigorously. Using the latest versions on February 23, 1964,

Richard Petty laps the #7 Ford driven by Bobby Johns in the 1964 Firecracker 400, thanks to the Hemi and the smaller frontal area of the 1964 Plymouth B-Body design. (Ray Mann Photo, Courtesy Cal Lane)

Don White's newly released fastback 1966 Dodge Charger was perhaps the first to truly benefit from subtle changes learned by the Special Vehicles Group. (Ray Mann Photo, Courtesy Cal Lane)

Richard Petty led Jimmy Pardue and Paul Goldsmith to a 1-2-3 finish for Plymouth at the Daytona 500.

In stock car racing, Chrysler's chief competitor was Ford Motor Company, as General Motors had formally dropped out in 1963. Ford had stuck with full-size cars, and partway through the 1963 model year, the company released a newly updated version of the Galaxie XL with a restyled roof shape and sloped rear roofline. Although it was not a true fastback to the rear valance, this fastback execution was for the direct benefit of downforce at circle track speeds. Credit therefore deserves to be given to this Total Performance 1963½ Galaxie and the associated Mercury Marauder as the first true hint of what became the 1960s aero-wars between Ford and Chrysler.

Chrysler actually had taken a different tack. The Dodge and Plymouth B-Body designs had been revised for 1964, featuring a narrower, lower, and shorter profile than the full-size Ford. They also featured flush grille work and a backswept rear cab design fitted with either slanted or curved glass. Because no other formal roofline was offered beyond a hardtop or pillarless coupe layout, there was no declaration of the car's inherent aero efficiencies. However, the history of Chrysler in

NASCAR for 1964 and the legacy of the new 426 Hemi might have been a bit different had these things not been coupled to that engine's introduction.

The differences became a source of contention between the companies as well as the sanctioning body. At the end of 1964, France decided to ban the Hemi as a non-production engine as well as force Chrysler to run full-size bodies. Householder called his bluff and boycotted the series for 1965. After France relented due to the Street Hemi's upcoming release, Ford boycotted NASCAR for part of 1966. Nevertheless, the aero wars continued.

In 1966, Dodge released a new fastback model called the Charger, which did take the rear cab slope literally to the back bumper. The problem was lift. Because the air sailed directly off this surface, the air wanted to pull the back of the car off the ground at higher speeds. The solution was a small deck-mounted spoiler that created enough downforce to address the problem. It gave Sam McQuagg's Charger a victory at Daytona's Firecracker 400 that summer and David Pearson won the 1966 Grand National championship. The Plymouth Belvedere, such as the one Richard Petty drove, appeared to be a box on wheels. However, it could be "raked" to

Richard Petty's Belvedere won the 1967 Grand National title; shown here in restored form outside at the Petty Museum. (Photo Courtesy Quartermilestones.com)

during drafting (when cars were close together at more than 170 mph), the company decided to begin aero-testing in two facilities. The scaled-down wind tunnel at Wichita State University in Kansas and Lockheed's full-size aircraft development tunnel in Georgia were rented, and the first cars involved were the 1968 models of the Charger and the Road Runner.

help downforce, and held its own well. Petty won the Daytona 500 in the rain the previous winter.

By now, Chrysler had begun studying scientifically provable aerodynamic ideas. Working in a Special Vehicles Group started in 1964 under Larry Rathgeb, John Pointer left the company's missile group and government work to join them. Bob Marcell arrived from the aerospace research lab at the University of Michigan. George Wallace, who possessed a brilliant mind and who played a pivotal role in this era of Chrysler's racing effort, was also there, along with Dick Lajoie, John Vaughn, and others.

Even though the 1967 Belvedere did not appear as slick as the Fords or Dodges, with gentle massaging here and there, it was slick enough, and Richard Petty was plenty talented. He won 27 races that season, including a string of 10 consecutive, and sealed the legacy of King Richard in NASCAR lore. Petty won the championship, Dodge won 5 other race titles, and Jim Paschal won 4 more for Plymouth, giving Chrysler 36 wins on the 49-race tour.

WIND TUNNELS

With superspeedway speeds now requiring more direct understanding, especially about what occurred

The stylists were rightly proud of their new Charger, with its inset and blacked-out grille, which looked like a big spaceship intake. To make room for the trunk, the rear window slanted steeply off the roofline between two long roof-to-body extensions. From the side, they made the car appear to be a fastback. The wind tunnel work showed that the grille was indeed a big scoop, and gave the Charger a lift rate of 1,250 pounds as air tried to escape from underneath the car. Meanwhile, the back window, with its flying buttress edges, caused air to shoot upward off the surface, working (quite literally) to pull the rear wheels off of the ground.

Bob McCurry, who headed Dodge at the time, wanted a winner. The stylists were not happy with seeing their work changed, but in spring 1968, McCurry approved a redesign called the 1969 Charger 500. This used a 1968-type Coronet grille to make the front of the car flush and a plug along with a much smaller deck lid to angle the rear window to the same angle that the bodyline flowed from the roof. The name was given for two reasons. The first was for its debut at Daytona for the 1969 season. The second was that the Automobile Competition Committee for the United States (ACCUS), the governing body of motorsports rules making, stated that a minimum quantity of 500 units of a given model must be built to be legal.

The new 1969 Charger 500 with its fastback window was announced in mid-1968 for a debut at the 1969 Daytona 500; the Fords proved to be a bit quicker and Dodge returned to the drawing board. Tim and Pam Wellborn formerly owned this Hemi example. (Photo Courtesy Quartermilestones.com)

The 1969 Ford Talladega was the reason Richard Petty made a one-season switch to Ford blue. Otherwise, Plymouth would not have committed the resources in late 1969 to build a truly competitive race car. (Photo Courtesy Quartermilestones.com)

For Richard Petty, 1968 proved to be a somewhat bittersweet follow-up to his dominating 1967 season. Ford released a new fastback called the Torino; Mercury offered an associated model named Cyclone. With less frontal area than Chryslers, they were slick enough to dominate most of the year. The wind tunnel work on Petty's 1968 Road Runner showed that it was competitive thanks to its own flush grille and rear window.

Therefore, when the Charger 500 was announced in June, he asked Plymouth what they planned to do for 1969.

The response was, "Nothing." Plymouth felt that the Road Runner was already a good fit and believed that Petty could still win in it. Ford, meanwhile, had just announced and received ACCUS approval for a newly designed aero styling package for the Torino called Talladega, named for a new NASCAR track Bill France was constructing in Alabama. This car (and companion Cyclone Spoiler) took the functionality a step further, with a deliberately dropped and extended nose and smoothed-out rear cab design.

Petty was now more alarmed and requested to move to Dodge to run a Charger 500 for the upcoming season. Neither Dodge, who had enough big-name drivers already, nor Plymouth, who frankly had no other big-name drivers, were interested in this change. Phone calls were made to Dearborn, contracts were let, and at the end of the 1968 season, Petty Enterprises announced that the number 43 would be on a Ford for 1969. Plymouth had no back-up plan for this consequence.

WINGS AND "THE SUMMER OF '69"

For Bob McCurry, it was the hope that Dodge could finally win the Daytona crown. He had a car, the Charger 500. He had four drivers: Bobby Isaac in the Harry Hyde #71, Buddy Baker in Ray Fox's #3, Cotton Owens's #6 driven by Chargin' Charlie Glotzbach, and Paul Goldsmith in Ray Nichels's shop car #9. Alas, LeeRoy Yarbrough, in a Torino Talladega owned by Junior Johnson, won by inches when Glotzbach could not pass him on the final lap. Bob McCurry was not happy. At all.

During the run-up to the event, John Pointer and Bob Marcell had each sketched out the next generation car in theory. Convention did not matter; only function mattered. The plan was to add a quite pointed nose rather than one that simply sloped. In addition, instead of a small deck spoiler, they wanted one of enough consequence to literally plant the back end of the car to the racetrack. With McCurry on the warpath, they showed him the rudimentary ideas.

"It's ugly," he reportedly said to the aerostylists, then added, "Will it win?"

They told him, "Yes, it would."

That settled, he gave it his final approval, and it was a no-holds-barred chase for its release. Work began in earnest using everything learned in the Charger 500 program to add an extended nose and figure out the spoiler design. This became more critical when noting that ACCUS intended to meet in late April 1969 to re-evaluate production numbers.

A number of things were discovered during this development process. Once the nose was configured properly, a set of front fender scoops was authorized for tire clearance, but they actually functioned more as air extractors. The rear wing was designed with an inverted Clark Y-style aircraft horizontal spoiler. It was styled high enough to clear the open deck lid. Using a pair of rear-fender-mounted streamlined uprights actually made this wing even more functional; the upright's slab-sided shape was capable of straightening out the car in the event of drifting or air speed coming from anywhere but the front.

The requisite number was again 500, with six months advance notice given. As a result, the new

The next step forward was a moonshot; the 1969 Charger Daytona looked like nothing that had ever appeared from any manufacturer. This Omaha Orange example, in the vicinity of an airplane propeller, was once in the Wellborn Museum's collection. (Photo Courtesy Quartermilestones.com)

The cartoon on the wing notwithstanding, Plymouth's Superbird was all business. (Photo Courtesy Quartermilestones.com)

Charger Daytona was formally introduced and shown to the press in the middle of April, with the implicit desire to have it debut at the new Talladega track in mid-September. ACCUS ruled mere weeks later that the new minimums going forward were one unit for every two dealerships.

The Daytona was truly an exercise in function; its look also had novelty and Dodge rode that wave into its dealerships as the cars began to show up in the latter half of 1969. Created from the normal Charger R/T packaging, all Daytonas were Hemi- or 440 Magnum–powered. In most cases they offered minimal extra options and base sold for little more than the conventional Charger R/T.

To facilitate construction as quickly as possible, Dodge turned to a Detroit-area fabrication firm, Creative Industries. Having worked on the Charger 500 program as well, Creative was tasked with constructing and installing the noses and wings, and making other changes to Charger R/Ts created on the assembly line. This included a large wraparound rear "scat stripe" that

read "DAYTONA." Working with engineer Dale Reeker from Chrysler, the parts were rapidly designed and all production issues dealt with quickly. Some immediate problems cropped up from the stylists, until McCurry stepped in and told them to shut up and back off. The Daytona arrived in time to help inaugurate the first race run at the Alabama International Motor Speedway in Talladega. It also won there.

Meanwhile, although Richard Petty had won a couple of races in his new Ford, it was not a great romance. Like Dodge, Ford had its own share of superstars, and they tended to get preferential treatment. The Petty team's long experience with Chrysler Hemi engines no doubt aided them as Ford's new Boss 429 had also arrived for 1969, and having the aero-styled Torino body was likely better than trying to tool around at 180 mph in a Road Runner, even if that vehicle had been named *Motor Trend*'s Car of the Year in 1969.

When Petty made statements that life was not perfect, Plymouth quickly got the hint. In June, some Chrysler people made quiet inquiries as to whether Mr. Petty would be interested in discussing a future back with Plymouth. He would. If they built a competitive aero-model, he would come back, but there would be a cost. In addition to money for racing Plymouths again, Petty Enterprises would also receive the corporation's entire circle track parts distribution and contract-racing business for which Ray Nichels/Paul Goldsmith were currently responsible. The authorization for that change reportedly went all the way to Chairman of the Board Lynn Townsend, who signed off on it.

The new ACCUS minimum requirement meant that Plymouth needed to build almost 2,000 units. Changes in federal headlamp laws, slated to go into effect on January 1, 1970, meant that the Daytona-type concealed headlamp design had to be off the assembly line before then. The stylists intended to get some comeuppance for Dodge's indiscretions, and took some. To top it off, the company had just six months to pull it all off.

The result was the Plymouth Superbird.

CHAPTER 2

BUILDING BIGGER 'BIRDS

A "flock" of Superbirds at a Mopar show in St. Louis. Sold under option A13, these cars were all built with standard equipment upgrades and deletes, becoming unique collector cars today. (Photo Courtesy Quartermilestones.com)

The Plymouth Superbird being built as a production model could only have happened during the era in which it was actually created. The amount of money, time, and frustration expended is almost shocking, but it reveals once again that Chrysler was all in when it came to special vehicle programs related to racing, as well as overcoming the problems associated with them. In this chapter, I discuss both the basic development of the Superbird as a potential production car and the challenges that creating more than 1,900 examples on the production line presented.

The exact date that initial development on Plymouth's wing actually began is unknown. It is probable that rough-drawn designs were played with a little before the company even talked with Richard Petty in June 1969. Although subcontractor Creative Industries of Detroit did not build the cars, in the end it was Chrysler engineers and stylists in that firm's offices who played a primary role in getting the project from theory to functionality. Frank Moriarty laid the initial groundwork for understanding this project in his books *Supercars* (out of print) and *Top Speed*.

It was this redesign of the 1970 Coronet's front sheet metal that helped Plymouth finalize plans for the Superbird, which used the Dodge fenders and a modified version of the hood

John Herlitz, manager of Plymouth's intermediate design studio, later recalled that his introduction to this program occurred when the race group contacted him to come to Creative and look at a proposal for a winged Plymouth, which was initially noted as the Belvedere-Daytona. Herlitz was already an unflattering critic of the radical treatment given to the Charger Daytona. He noted immediately that changes were necessary from this initial concept to make the ideas more palatable to the general buying public.

For example, it had been hoped that Dodge Charger fenders could in some way be adapted to the Belvedere-Daytona. Because of the Plymouth's bodylines, Herlitz immediately recognized that blending those two styles was impossible. However, Dodge had just redesigned the 1970 front clip for the Coronet line; it was slightly more rounded than before but similar to upcoming front sheet metal changes for the 1970 Belvedere line. Using those fenders and their associated hood was the first step to adding a streamlined nose to the Road Runner.

Despite initial hopes to the contrary, the Daytona nose (the beak) was going to need restyling after all. It would have to be slightly wider than the Charger

Daytona version. Although most parameters from the Daytona's nose design could be left intact, the stylists did not like the amount of droop on the Daytona version and asked that the front edge be brought up approximately 2 inches in the interest of appearance. This change increased the amount of drag at race speeds, but no argument could be made because so many cars needed to be sold to the public.

To adapt the Coronet's hood to the nose required adding a special front fill panel as well as a redesigned front valance (under the grille area). The steel lower

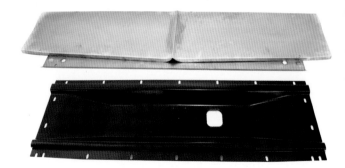

The added fill section for the hood, lower spoiler, and new hood latch tray specific to all Superbirds is shown here. (Photo Courtesy ricksparts.net)

front spoiler that was used on the Daytona as well as a pair of injection-molded plastic rear-facing front fender scoops over the wheel housings were already optimized for cooling. The factory paperwork simply called them air scoops. However, the aero stylists quietly noted that they were for race-speed air extraction due to nose downforce. It was often rumored that they were

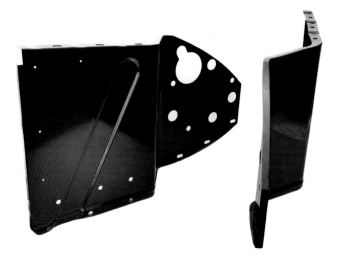

These multi-angled sections were nose support pieces mounted behind the front fender on each side of the car. (Photo Courtesy ricksparts.net)

Here is the completed nose, showing the hood extension, standard-equipment J45 pin layout, and steel lower spoiler. (Photo Courtesy Quartermilestones.com)

for tire clearance or brake cooling. Herlitz designed black graphics for the headlamp doors; additional aero improvements came from wide, chrome edge-trim attached to the windshield A-pillars.

To make the headlights work, they used the vacuum canister Charger-type cover operation. However, the real issue was related to upcoming Federal Motor Vehicle Safety Standards (FMVSS) on the functionality of concealed headlamps in the event of equipment problems (believed to be Sec 571.112 – S4.1-4.2 of the FMVSS code). Chrysler employee and drag racer John Tedder told me that this was a specific reason for the completion of the cars before the new year. In addition, another problem crept up when the state of Maryland refused to title the cars under any circumstances because they didn't have a visible front bumper. A rumor persists that the company actually had to buy back these cars.

OUT BACK

The Road Runner was never offered in a fastback form. Moreover, to prevent costs from spiraling further upward, no changes could be made to the C-pillar location or the "Dutchman panel" used between the rear window opening and the trunk lip sheet metal as on the Charger 500 and Daytona. As a result, aerodynamicist Dick Lajoie and others did extensive testing on possible window reworkings using the rented Wichita State University's 3/8-scale wind tunnel and eventually settled on a rear area metal plug and lightly restyled rear window glass. This change was not as good as true fastbacking would have been. It also made a black vinyl top mandatory on all Superbirds to hide this change.

Herlitz also wanted the rear wing restyled. As a result, the uprights were wider, canted farther inboard, and swept more rearward than the Daytona version. In this case, there was actually added aero benefit to the redesign because the increased shape made the car more stable in racing traffic.

By approximately the end of July, the costs of these

Out back, an aero-styled plug was added to the car atop the standard Road Runner stamping, requiring that all Superbirds receive a vinyl top. (Photo Courtesy Quartermilestones.com)

This is a regular 1970 Road Runner backlight with optional vinyl top, showing the original styling cues that required a special body-paint corner trim molding to match after the plug was added. (Photo Courtesy Quartermilestones.com)

This Superbird, currently under restoration by Dale Mathews, shows how the backlight was mounted against the original window opening, precluding the need to cut out the OEM stamping.

changes were finally evaluated. Publically, Dodge had estimated a loss of $1,500 on each of the 500 Daytonas built, which had a base price of $3,993. Although the actual Plymouths' costs were never released, it would be safe to say that it cost the company at least the same amount, even if the base cost of a Superbird with a standard 440 4-barrel engine had been pushed to $4,298. In fact, despite the commitment in time and money already expended, Plymouth pulled the plug on the entire project in early August, reportedly due to the then-projected costs associated with production. However, the cancellation was rescinded two weeks later. The show would indeed go on, and without a moment to spare.

Creative Industries's people worked closely with Chrysler to quickly mock-up the finalized parts, get initial samples done, and begin subcontracting the work. Although they had leased a substantial facility on 10 Mile Road, changing almost 2,000 cars to the degree that the Superbird required was out of the question, especially in the time allowed. Chrysler's Lynch Road plant in Hamtramck, Michigan, became the location for all initial Superbird construction, with final assembly completed at an associated pre-production pilot facility on nearby Clairpointe Street. The facility was normally used to check tooling and fitment issues for each upcoming model year. All 1970 pilot work was long completed by October 1969 and the 1971 pilot model process did not begin until spring 1970. The plant was large enough to do the job, factory-owned, and it was nearby. That settled the issue.

For its part, Creative Industries was responsible for creating or procuring all the specific components that would be used on the Superbird. The wing, small add-ons, front spoiler, and fully constructed nose assemblies came through them. It was a huge undertaking based on how quickly the cars would be going into production. Thankfully, all internal components from the Daytona nose were adapted unaltered to the Superbird version. The nose structure on both cars was always steel with the headlamp doors being the only fiberglass components.

Factory paperwork in the Frank Badalson and David Patik collections shows that the first documentation summary for Plymouth NASCAR Program tools and special equipment was announced via interoffice correspondence on August 18. It cryptically alluded to success only if the program was reactivated by August 20. This denoted component materials, initial supply dates, and tooling times (most by early September, with some as late as October 8).

Next, an August 25, 1969, meeting at Creative with Scott Harvey and L. B. Wiser of Product Planning got things moving by delineating some preliminary ideas regarding actual construction; this determined which locations would handle certain parts of the process. It is now believed that this proposal was later modified via a document dated October 21, 1969 (pages 28–30). This Plymouth NASCAR Check List is a Lynch Road production-line check sheet showing exactly what would occur during each step from the initial body-in-white to the final line details. Interoffice mail dated October 7 gave the formal release notification of the special car package to all plant management under SO B30 J97000 J99499.

ON TO LYNCH ROAD

To understand how the Superbird was built, you need an introductory understanding of the production process. In 1969, a Chrysler product's origins began through Production Scheduling when the build data was first input into the company's corporate mainframe computer. This data came from an order via either a dealer or through corporate channels based on current or future market demand for that model. With every order entered, each car was assigned its VIN. Due to their special nature, all Superbird construction was scheduled for Lynch Road, so the issue became one of proper sequencing to keep the assembly line moving during the nine or so weeks of building the cars in the final months of 1969.

At Lynch Road, which was 660 feet wide and 2,500 feet long, the assembly process was divided into several steps and flow areas: Metal, Paint, Trim, Chassis, and Final Lines plus sub-assembly and repair areas. A document by expert David Patik, "Lynch Road Assembly Plant Tour," is invaluable in understanding how this worked. On the line, different bodies and styles were deliberately interspersed to allow examples with standard equipment to be completed quickly and spend additional line time on models with more options. Therefore, even if original VIN sequencing may have been close, the actual spacing on the assembly line could have been farther apart.

Hemi-powered cars were their own breed due to unique component work and standardized body extras, and it's believed that only one or two were built per shift due to their special attention. The plant normally

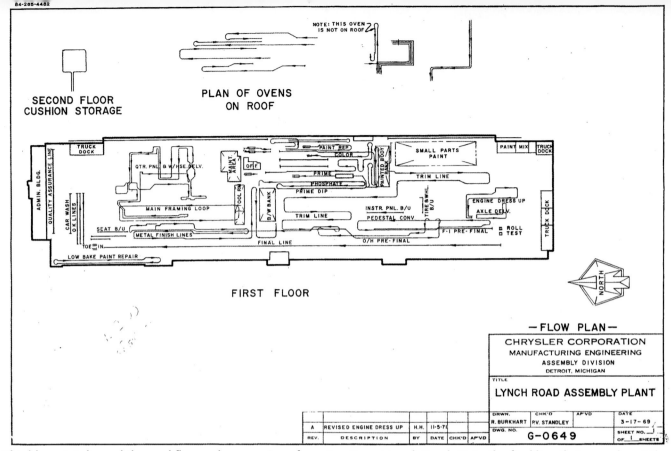

SECOND FLOOR
CUSHION STORAGE

PLAN OF OVENS
ON ROOF

NOTE: THIS OVEN
IS NOT ON ROOF

FIRST FLOOR

— FLOW PLAN —

CHRYSLER CORPORATION
MANUFACTURING ENGINEERING
ASSEMBLY DIVISION
DETROIT, MICHIGAN

TITLE

LYNCH ROAD ASSEMBLY PLANT

REV.	DESCRIPTION	BY	DATE	CHK'D	AP'VD
A	REVISED ENGINE DRESS UP	H.H.	11-5-71		

DRWN.	CHK'D	AP'VD	DATE
R. BURKHART	P.V. STANDLEY		3-17-69

DWG. NO. G-0649

SHEET NO.
OF   1   SHEETS

This blueprint showed the workflow and sequencing of construction at Lynch Road. Note the final line that runs almost the whole length of the plant. (Drawing Courtesy David Patik Collection)

This aerial view shows the sprawling Lynch Road assembly plant in Detroit. (Dodge, Plymouth, and the AMC design are registered trademarks of FCA US LLC.)

pushed out the equivalent of one car per *minute* during two eight-hour shifts each day during this period, although the entire construction process for a car from start to finish was approximately two days.

For Superbird construction at its maximum of approximately 50 units per day, it portends that one 'Bird was started every 20 minutes or so, likely using additional metal workers to do the many small fixture changes required. The early document released in August suggested that the cars be sent to Clairpointe Street for the special backlight plug and welding, returned to Lynch Road for paint, and then sent back to Clairpointe Street for final finishing. The subsequent internal Plymouth NASCAR Check List dated shortly after production began on October 21, 1969, shows all metalwork was actually being done in Lynch Road's Metal Shop.

METAL SHOP

The Patik paperwork gave a hypothetical Superbird a trip through the plant as follows; after the production was scheduled by date, the order first went to the Metal (Body) Shop. Here, pre-formed sheet metal stampings already on hand based to the scheduled production window were welded together to create the basic car structure. Using a floor-level fixture, or gate, to locate the crucial framework and subassemblies, the initial structure of the car first came together. The body VINs were also stamped on at this point.

In the Metal Shop, the rear window plug specific to the Superbird was added on. To do this, the body structure was pushed into a sidetrack area off the main body line to keep the line moving; special instructions were given on welding in the new backlight atop the standard opening. Other metal Superbird components welded in or added here included the rear wing support pads under the rear quarter panel tops, jack brace brackets in the trunk, and the bracket for the special hood-latch tray.

The car was placed back on the main line to con-

Assembly-line photography was carefully guarded and was not common in the public domain. This image from 1967 at Lynch Road shows a Coronet being built. Various broadcast sheets assist in making sure the equipment added is correct. (Dodge, Plymouth, and the AMC design are registered trademarks of FCA US LLC.)

tinue toward the Paint Shop. A fender tag was added to the car, held by one forward screw so it could be lifted and marked by inspectors as needed, or hung onto the car by a wire. In the case of Hemi Superbirds, the N96 fresh air (Air Grabber) option was almost always X'd out by inspectors because the Hemi option used it as standard equipment; none were available on Superbirds. The tag's second screw was put in place later, which is why it is sometimes unpainted.

Continuing on, the Coronet fenders were installed as normal bolt-on components and any holes specific to each vehicle's options were drilled open in the body structure. On the Superbird, these included the mounting holes for the fender air scoops and wing and specific holes for the headlight vacuum-hose routing. The hood, already modified with an extension from the Coronet design by Chrysler's stamping plant, was placed on the structure, as was the Road Runner deck lid and the doors, which were standard. Some opening components were held in place by small recyclable wire latches.

Chrysler kept no record of how many Superbirds were painted in each color. The percentages given in the captions are courtesy of Galen Govier's research and represent averages based on existing cars in the Chrysler Registry. Also noted are extra-cost paint and decal colors.

The prepped body surface was sprayed with enamel by a combination of automated sprayers and handheld guns. It was then baked for permanence, its quality care-

Vitamin "C" Orange EK2, approximately 16 percent, extra-cost High Impact paint, used a white Plymouth decal.

Blue Fire Metallic EB5, approximately 14 percent, used a white Plymouth decal.

Tor-Red EV2, approximately 14 percent, used a white Plymouth decal.

Alpine White EW1, approximately 17 percent, used a black Plymouth decal.

Lemon Twist FY1, approximately 23 percent, extra-cost High Impact paint, used a black Plymouth decal.

Lime Light FJ5, approximately 11 percent, extra-cost High Impact paint; most used a black Plymouth decal, some used white.

fully checked for runs and sags, and redone if necessary. Once approved, the painted shell with no additional components moved to a temporary indoor storage area where it was deliberately sequenced into the Trim Line

with other mixed vehicles to keep the line continually moving. In an area of the paint shop, the mandated vinyl top was installed, an always-black custom-cut version because of the rear window design.

Corporate (Petty) Blue 999, approximately 5 percent, used a white Plymouth decal.

Burnt Orange Metallic FK5, approximately .1 percent (less than 10 examples), used a white Plymouth decal. (Steve Reyes Photo)

PAINTING BY NUMBERS

The car went into a holding area to be sequenced into the Paint Shop. Using hooks for movement and support, this multi-step process included a thorough cleaning of the assembled body, pre-conditioning treatments, and an initial body dip into primer (to headlight level), among others. The Superbird again required unique attention during this process; a workman used Plastisol body filler to clean up the backlight plug fitment edges, eliminating the need for lead filler. Other body sealers and sound deadener went on as well, and the car was primed again in spray, with the doors and upper lids held in place.

Any interior color paint (limited to either black or white for Superbird models) was now spot-added to those surfaces not covered by upholstery in the interior area, and this was usually done before the second prime coat was dry. The entire body structure was then baked to finalize the pretreatment.

By this point in most cases, any component now receiving the actual body color was fitted onto the car; with a Superbird, however, the wing, front fender scoops, and nose were not. In addition, the special side valances for mating the fenders to the nose, which could not be added because no nose was on the car, were hung by wires inside the interior to be painted the body color with the car.

Painted earlier, the interior was then masked off to prevent overspray. From its outside supplier, the cast rear window corner trim (from the outside supplier) arrived finished in one of the Superbird's seven available body colors, which meant that the high-potential-for-rust area beneath those corners was still open. After the joints were properly soldered, this area was also paint-finished during this process, and the cast corner moldings were added during the Final Line assembly.

The car was now ready for its assigned color, coded as follows on the fender tag: EB5, EW1, EK2, FY1, FJ5,

EV2, and 999 (Special Order Corporate/Petty Blue). Due to the unique body color subassemblies required for Superbird, this much-shorter list differed from the standard Road Runner colors, and even then, a few FK5 examples were created, likely to the hair-tearing chagrin of line managers.

TRIM AND CHASSIS LINE

Although the basic body was done, the actual construction plans for this car started sometime earlier. Once the day's management tracking sheet had been generated showing all the cars listed by VIN entering from this staging area onto the Trim Line, each car build-up was mixed into a specific plant sequence for actual production. This means that everything from a 6-cylinder torsion bar to a Hemi engine was ready to go onto that car as soon as it came to that specific area in the line.

Every part was designated to make both identification and installation easy, hence the tape stripes or paint dabs specific to certain components. Furthermore, multiple copies of the resultant broadcast (or build) sheets were also created in exact order for every single car. These sheets were printed via a teletype computer printer located in each line area, ensuring no surprises as the shell moved forward.

Once a body started moving down the Trim Line, the wiring and electrical components, rubber seals, and the pre-assembled dash layout were installed. This trim was actually the raw components of the car. Of course, the Superbird did not have headlights installed here as a normal car did, but everything to activate them, such as vacuum canister and lines, wiring, etc., was added. Indeed, all non-driveline equipment preparing the body for initial start-up and roller testing was installed on the Trim Line.

Simultaneous to the body moving through Trim, its designated engine, shown on the identical broadcast sheet printed in that area, entered into Chassis Assembly from the plant's supply stable. The new engine had

A Hemi cutaway engine in the Garlits museum shows its internal parts. Engines going into cars on the assembly line were "run in" at the engine plant using propane. Carburetors were installed at Lynch Road as the engine moved toward its car.

already been test-run at the engine plant using propane and therefore was not yet carbureted.

First, the specific VIN for its car was stamped on the engine, and it was mated to the appropriate transmission, which was also VIN-stamped. Next, all missing components including carb(s), linkages, fan, oil sending unit, speedometer pinion, etc. (but not the air cleaner), were added.

Working on a carousel layout, the assembled engine/transmission set was placed on a moving line and settled into the proper K-frame. The front suspension and brake assemblies were also being completed and built into a full subassembly around this. A ready-built differential assembly, tagged with its ratio and taped or painted for easy identification, was also placed on the line here, spaced exactly right for mounting points to the body and with shocks and springs properly located. The Chassis Line did for the drivetrain what the Trim Line did for the body.

Another 1967 image from Lynch Road shows B-bodies coming off the Final Line for inspection; Superbirds have shown up here minus nose and ready for movement to Clairpointe Street for final assembly. (Dodge, Plymouth, and the AMC design are registered trademarks of FCA US LLC.)

Always moving as work continued, the Chassis Line, located at a lower point in the plant, now rose and made a union with the Trim Line, where the Superbird body could be dropped down over it. Major parts were tightened up, linkages and fuel lines attached, fluids added, and the entire car now rose from the floor on what was called the High Line to allow installation of the wheels and tires, including the steel-rim spare.

Once complete and riding on its own wheels, the noseless Superbird moved to the line's end, where somebody popped a plastic seat or wooden box into it as a temporary driver's perch and started it for the first time. It was then driven a short distance to the Rolls, where the new engine was run under varying conditions on rear-wheel chassis rollers and had other components tested for acceptance; anything rejected here went to a nearby repair area to be fixed. Nothing was scrapped that made it this far in the process.

If these checks proved to be satisfactory, the car was moved to the Final Line, which ran a full 1,800-foot length of the plant floor. Here it received the interior, including the specific black-only Superbird headliner (again, custom cut because of the rear window), and

glass. It was then spray water-tested to guarantee sealing, and if that was okay, the interior and carpet were added.

The broadcast sheet generated in the nearby interior subassembly area, placed into a seat back or seat springs, usually shows up when doing a vehicle tear-down today. Other than that and the example sometimes placed above the glove box during dash subassembly, the rest were usually discarded in the trash during the car's construction.

Meanwhile, people were also working in a centered pit below the Final Line; the torsion bars, steering, and suspension were final-adjusted. The standard jack was added; small trim and chrome went on, including the special A-pillar chrome and painted cast rear window corners. If special graphics or items were needed, the car came off the line and into an adjacent cubbyhole for special treatment. Superbirds were not part of that group because graphics were added at Clairpointe Street. As it arrived at the end of the Final Line, spray-on paint wax protectant and the Lynch Road plant-generated Monroney label (window sticker) were the last things added before the car left the building.

OUT THE DOOR, DOWN THE STREET

Most vehicles coming out of the building were stored briefly then loaded onto trucks or railcars for dealer shipment. The still-incomplete 'Birds were quickly placed in truckload batches on semitrailers for the ride over to Clairpointe Street, about 5 miles away. According to existing records, the Superbirds were not completed in any sequence. The first one leaving Clairpointe Street was 149789 (October 17 and used as the prototype); the last group shipped out on December 18 range randomly from 179754 to 181254, yet the actual known Superbird VIN numbers range between 149789 and 181274. Incidentally, unit 9789 was a V-code Six Pack and was the fifth example built on the Lynch Road line.

Although they were finished as quickly as possible,

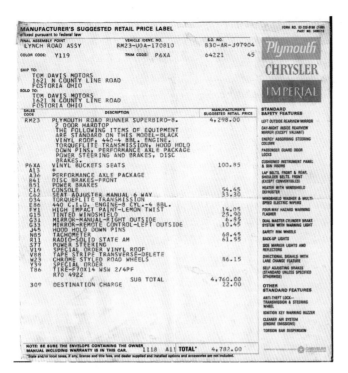

FINAL ASSEMBLY POINT	VEHICLE IDENT. NO.	S.O. NO.	
LYNCH ROAD ASSY	RM23-U0A-170810	B30-AR-J97904	*Plymouth*
COLOR CODE: Y119	TRIM CODE: P6XA	64221 45	CHRYSLER
			IMPERIAL

SHIP TO:
TOM DAVIS MOTORS
1621 N COUNTY LINE ROAD
FOSTORIA OHIO
SOLD TO:
TOM DAVIS MOTORS
1621 N COUNTY LINE ROAD
FOSTORIA OHIO

SALES CODE	DESCRIPTION	MANUFACTURER'S SUGGESTED RETAIL PRICE	STANDARD SAFETY FEATURES
RM23	PLYMOUTH ROAD RUNNER SUPERBIRD-8.	4,298.00	LEFT OUTSIDE REARVIEW MIRROR
	2 DOOR HARDTOP		DAY-NIGHT INSIDE REARVIEW MIRROR (EXCEPT VALIANT)
	THE FOLLOWING ITEMS OF EQUIPMENT ARE STANDARD ON THIS MODEL-BLACK VINYL ROOF, 440-4 BBL. ENGINE TORQUEFLITE TRANSMISSION, HOOD HOLD DOWN PINS, PERFORMANCE AXLE PACKAGE POWER STEERING AND BRAKES, DISC BRAKES.		ENERGY ABSORBING STEERING COLUMN
			PASSENGER GUARD DOOR LOCKS
P6XA	VINYL BUCKETS SEATS	100.85	CUSHIONED INSTRUMENT PANEL & SUN VISORS
A13	*		LAP BELTS, FRONT & REAR, SHOULDER BELTS, FRONT (EXCEPT CONVERTIBLES)
A36	PERFORMANCE AXLE PACKAGE		
B41	DISC BRAKES-FRONT		
B51	POWER BRAKES	54.45	HEATER WITH WINDSHIELD DEFROSTER
C16	CONSOLE	53.30	
C62	SEAT ADJUSTER MANUAL 6 WAY		WINDSHIELD WASHER & MULTI-SPEED ELECTRIC WIPERS
D34	TORQUEFLITE TRANSMISSION		
E86	440 C.I.D. ENGINE-8 CYL.-4 BBL.		FOUR-WAY HAZARD WARNING FLASHER
FY1	HIGH IMPACT PAINT-LEMON TWIST	14.05	
G15	TINTED WINDSHIELD	25.90	DUAL MASTER CYLINDER BRAKE SYSTEM WITH WARNING LIGHT
G31	MIRROR-MANUAL-RIGHT OUTSIDE	6.85	
G33	MIRROR-REMOTE CONTROL-LEFT OUTSIDE	10.45	SAFETY RIM WHEELS
J45	HOOD HOLD DOWN PINS		BACK-UP LIGHTS
N85	TACHOMETER	68.45	
R11	RADIO-SOLID STATE AM	61.55	SIDE MARKER LIGHTS AND REFLECTORS
S77	POWER STEERING		
V19	SPECIAL ORDER VINYL ROOF		DIRECTIONAL SIGNALS WITH LANE CHANGE FEATURE
V88	TAPE STRIPE TRANSVERSE-DELETE		
W23	CHROME STYLED ROAD WHEELS	86.15	SELF ADJUSTING BRAKES (STANDARD UNLESS SPECIFIED OTHERWISE)
Y59	SPECIAL ORDER		
T86	TIRE-F70X14 WSW 2/4PF		OTHER STANDARD FEATURES
	R70 4922		ANTI-THEFT LOCK- TRANSMISSION & STEERING WHEEL
	SUB TOTAL	4,760.00	
309	DESTINATION CHARGE	22.00	IGNITION KEY WARNING BUZZER
			CLEANER AIR SYSTEM (ENGINE EMISSIONS)
			TORSION BAR SUSPENSION

The last step was to attach a Monroney sticker such as this to the car, denoting the options as built on the assembly line. (Photo Courtesy Frank Badalson)

some may have been held back for a more appropriate time for completion and perhaps a handful were incorrectly built; at least one is believed to have gone back to Lynch Road for major repair work. Beyond that, Superbirds were likely completed based on either their physical location to the Clairpointe Street plant entrance or in scheduled batched groupings to facilitate the quickest-possible assembly.

Despite their incomplete appearance as delivered from Lynch Road, these running Plymouths were actually almost finished. All they required mechanically was that the preassembled noses be installed and headlamps hooked up and adjusted. Installation of the front turn signal lights (a Fury part) was also finished once the nose and front valances were added, the front spoiler and rear wing were mounted, and graphics were added, with the large Plymouth decals on the rear quarter panels added as the final touch.

The real issue between Lynch Road and Clairpointe Street was paint matching. Instead of enamel, the assembled noses were shot in lacquer because they could not be baked due to their componentry, and the color was not always an exact match to the car's similar

An amazing find from Brandt Rosenbusch at Chrysler Historical was this late 1969 aerial view of the Jefferson Avenue plant, Clairpointe Street facility, and associated plants. (Dodge, Plymouth, and the AMC design are registered trademarks of FCA US LLC.)

body hue; aging has made this even more evident in some cases. Likewise, the wing assembly parts and fender air scoops were also painted in lacquer body color.

According to the August prerelease information in Frank Badalson's paper collection, the noses were to be delivered in black primer. If so, these parts were painted and detailed at Clairpointe Street's facility based on whatever colors were needed for the car(s) being scheduled or completed at that time. If that is the case, it stands to reason that groups of Superbirds being finished at the Clairpointe Street plant were batched by color for final assembly. As a result, workers may have completed nose and wing parts for multiple examples (i.e., a group of Alpine White EW1 models) at one time. The fender scoops and lower valance were painted in Lynch Road's small parts area.

Final construction was still a fast turnaround as long as parts supply availability was not an issue (this was obviously crucial and avoided at all costs), with many cars believed to have been in and out of Clairpointe Street within 24 hours. They then returned to Lynch Road to be shipped to their final destination.

CONCLUSION

Building the number of Superbirds that Plymouth created in the short time span needed was an immense undertaking. It is likely that line workers were not thrilled to see all the special handling that these cars required, but they managed it. It has been noted that most Superbirds were sales bank cars, created primarily to make the cars available in the time frame allotted, then assigned to each region based on projected sales.

That said, I know of one Hemi example that was special-ordered with power windows and still owned by its originating 1969 sales-buyer as late as 2005. There were certainly other dealers who turned in their paperwork noting specific options by the time these cars were being built. Some of them were probably not in keeping with the factory protocols for this package (coded A13), but variations from the standard available/not available option lists, such as the FK5 painted cars or a rear stereo speaker, were very rare exceptions.

As a result of so many being built without pre-order, of the 1,935 units reportedly constructed, a vast majority

While few Superbirds were heavily optioned, salesman Smith Stokes ordered this Vitamin "C" Orange example with a Hemi and power windows in 1969. He later purchased it from the dealership, which he actually owned at the time. (Photo Courtesy Quartermilestones.com)

Ready for shipment from the Lynch Road plant, the Superbirds were ready for the world. But was the world ready for them? (Dodge, Plymouth, and the AMC design are registered trademarks of FCA US LLC.)

were engine-code A134 GTX-type 440 4-barrel powered, 618 automatics and 466 4-speeds, for a total of 1,084. It is now believed that 716 received the $119 440 6-barrel engine (408 autos, 308 4-speeds), and only 135 (77 automatics, 58 4-speeds) of the almost 2,000 cars eventually built found the $648.25 Hemi option under the hood.

The company had the cars. Now, the challenge was to find buyers for them.

```
                                          10-21-69


              PLYMOUTH NASCAR - CHECK LIST


    BODY-IN-WHITE

      1.  Backlight top reinforcement--spot weld to upper body and plug
          fence

      2.  Angular reinforcements top and sides tack welded to body and
          fusion welded to body and plug by bridging ½ weld at 3" spacing.

      3.  Anti-corrosion paint deck upper panel and plug surface at plug
          to drain trough joint.

      4.  Spot weld plug to deck upper each side and at drain trough.

      5.  CO² weld plug lower reinforcement to deck upper.

      6.  Three ¼" drain holes drilled in deck upper panel--one center
          and one each side.

      7.  Deck lid hinge stops welded to supports.

      8.  Jack stowage stud welded right side of trunk floor.

      9.  Four ½" holes for vertical fin drilled each quarter panel
          top surface.

     10.  Quarter panel reinforcements welded to each quarter drain
          trough; holes in quarter and reinforcement must align.

     11.  Fin vertical supports located in trunk right and left side
          with angle brackets welded to trunk floor side extensions.

     12.  "Road Runner" name plate holes in side of quarter panels to
          be omitted.

     13.  Deck lid "Road Runner" name holes required on cars not taking
          V8 stripe.

     14.  Quarter inch holes for vinyl top moulding and deck upper to
          plug joint moulding.

     15.  Roof to quarter joint soldered, except for rear 1", finish
          for vinyl top.

     16.  One 1-9/16 hole in dash for vacuum hoses  use 1-½ hole saw.

     17.  Two ¼" holes left fender side shield for vacuum tube retainers.

     18.  Two ¼" holes left side top of yoke for vacuum tube retainers.

     19.  Two  203 holes top of left rail ahead of shock tower for
          vacuum tank mounting.
```

Reproduced in the next three pages are the internal Lynch Road assembly instructions for body-in-white changes mandated for Superbird build-ups. They show the sequence of events to modify a standard Road Runner body to Superbird specifications. (Dodge, Plymouth, and the AMC design are registered trademarks of FCA US LLC.)

BODY-IN-WHITE

20. Drill hood and yoke for tie-down pins, same as J-45, (5) holes
    (4) 1/8 plus 1-1-1/8.

21. Bulkhead closure extension spot welded to yoke.

22. On cars with E-74 engine oil cooler mounting bracket welded
    to yoke, special "Nascar" type. (Auto. Trans. only)

23. On E-74 cars standard "Nascar" hood used, "Air Grabber" not
    available on "Nascar".

24. Fenders, modified Coronet type, top surface drilled
    (5, 9/32" holes) for air scoop mounting.

25. Solder front fender at nose to raise character line.

26. Drill one 3/16" dia. hole in H/L Mtg plate for attaching seal.

PAINT

1. Road Runner tail lamp paint treatment.

2. Plymouth quarter panel side marker bezels.

3. No fender bezels, takes Coronet chrome type.

4. Plug to quarter finish of die casting painted body color
   except for masked moulding section.

5. Black vinyl roof standard all jobs.

6. Vinyl seal all exposed seams of backlight plug to quarter
   and deck upper panel.

7. Seal area between quarter panel and plug below angular supports
   with foil tape.

HARDWARE - Instrument Panel

1. Road Runner type with 1969 Charger headlamp switch (2947807)
   with vacuum door actuating valve.

2. Vacuum tubes for headlamp door actuators.

3. No air conditioner, no Air Grabber... other,

4. Dash to yoke wiring harness (3571169).

5. Vacuum tank (2889965) mounted on rail below battery tray.

6. Vacuum tube grommet in dash.

7. Vacuum tubes clipped to left fender shield and left side of
   yoke.

8. Headlamp wiring passes over top of yoke and clipped with vacuum
   tubes to yoke.

HARDWARE - Instrument Panel cont'd.

9. Coronet front fender side markers, Belvedere rear quarter panel side markers.

10. Route trunk harness outboard of left stabilizer support and do not clip in center clip.

11. Install headlining retainers at backlight opening (3571182-3 and 126-7.

12. Air scoops mounted on top of fenders.

13. Cut and install fender headlamp plate seal.

HIGH LINE
1 Install side valance panel to fenders.

FLAT TOP

1. Cement yoke to radiator seals one top (1/2$\frac{1}{4}$) and one bottom (3/4") to radiator and install assembly to car.

CHASSIS - Coded items as specified

1. Vacuum fitting on engine (1944092)

2. Power steering pressure hose (2891185).

FINAL LINE

1. Special headlining and listing (3571103).

2. Special shelf trim panel (3571104).

3. One piece flexible garnish at backlight (3571105).

4. All cars take clear backlight (3571121).

5. Special backlight outside mouldings.

6. Streamlined "A" post outside mouldings (3412150-1) attached with two exposed screws, snap in behind roof rail weatherstrip retainer.

7. Install special (reworked) trunk mat.

CHESTER A. GARBACZ
Product Engineering Mgr.

CAG/ek

CHAPTER 3

MARKETING AND COMPETITION: HOW THE 'BIRDS FLEW

What a difference a year makes. Dr. Donald Tarr, who raced this Superbird only at the 1970 Firecracker 400, passes the 1969 Road Runner of Frank Warren on the high banks of the storied Daytona track. However, the aero-design fell to the rule-makers' pen for 1971, and some Plymouth dealers still had new ones on the lot. (Cal Lane Photo, Courtesy Ray Mann Archive)

In chapter 2, I explained how the Superbirds were constructed and why. As you'll see in this chapter, discounting Richard Petty's accident at Darlington, the Superbird might well have won NASCAR's Grand National series championship in 1970, which was why it was created. It did take crowns in both the Automobile Racing Club of America (ARCA) and the United States Auto Club (USAC) that season, as well as several major race titles, so it was not a failure in competition. Regardless, those accolades were not enough to make the cars a quick sale from dealership lots.

Buying any new car is a serious purchase, and although the performance marketplace was still burning as the cars arrived on dealer's lots, three factors hurt Superbird sales dramatically. The first was simply its appearance; as much as they are appreciated today, to some extent, any wing car fad had come and gone months earlier with the Dodge Daytonas, at least for new car buyers. This follow-up by Plymouth was perceived as simply another novelty in the era of Trans Am packages, special engine designs, and colorful graphics. Coupled with the Road Runner cartoon logos, its appeal to the sophisticated market buyer was minimal; those buyers were in the dealership for a 'Cuda or GTX at the same asking price for a Superbird.

Indeed, that played as the second factor. The 1970 model year saw huge changes in the lineups across Detroit. Chevrolet, Buick, and Olds now took top billing in the displacement wars thanks to new 454/455 engine options. Both General Motors and Ford had redesigns, as did Chrysler. Of course, the new E-Body 'Cuda was a focal point, but for Plymouth there was also the Duster and hot options such as the Air Grabber on Road Runner and GTX. Nobody was hurting for possible combinations that year, so Superbirds were not topping the desire list for most buyers from that standpoint, either.

The third factor made it a perfect storm. Work between Congress and the insurance industry had yielded statistical realities that performance cars posed greater possibilities of causing or being in an accident. As a result, starting in mid-1969, major underwriters began adding big surcharges to supercar purchases. In some cases and locales, that insurance payment equaled or was greater than the car payment. This reality shut out a lot of potential buyers from the big-block marketplace altogether. Subsequently, in 1970, the Plymouth 340-ci packages grew in popularity while brawlers such as the sales-bank-built 440-ci wing cars languished in the back of the lot.

There were other reasons as well, including emissions controls that began to take the edge off performance engineering, a questionable economy, and perhaps a desire for normalcy following the outrages of the 1960s. In the end, Plymouth dealers found that getting 'Birds to fly was difficult, regardless of what the blue #41 and #43 twins out of North Carolina were proving on the racetrack.

MARKETING IN GENERAL

The Superbird was featured in just two period Chrysler/Plymouth advertisements. Both were across-the-center spreads; one showed Richard Petty and the crew in their Level Cross race shop and the other showed a rustic barn and a group of bootleggers, supposedly in Tennessee. These ran primarily in automotive magazines and were produced only in black and white. Color ads in mainstream periodicals were reserved for the new Barracuda and larger cars. A handful of magazines ran press release reviews of the A13 wing, but very few actually drove the car, relying more on factory photos and information. Again,

It's a bird!
It's a car!
It's the Road Runner!
Superbird
from Plymouth's
Rapid Transit System!

The rare dealership-only brochure was the sole marketing tool created to sell the model. Black and white, it gave dealers reasons to have a 'Bird on display and basic information on available and unavailable options. No public marketing release for the program is known.

'Cuda and Duster got the most ink by testers for Plymouth's 1970 model line, with the B-Body tests reserved primarily for Road Runner and GTX. The Superbird's most visible appearance in the national automotive press was notable, however. It was the January 1970 cover of *Motor Trend*; Dan Gurney was sitting on the rear wing and a story inside told about the car's development.

The factory also created a single-sheet two-page foldout as the A13 cars were being scheduled for production. This item is also black and white and, based on its wording, was directed toward the dealer network rather than the general public. One statement reads, "The Superbird is no put-on. The car is a veritable self-propelled, self-liquidating, traffic builder." It was further noted that it could help bring in floor traffic to buy a more traditional performance model. Perhaps the company already sensed that there would be challenges to the sales effort.

As noted previously, there were not a lot of preorders; it is likely that any Hemi-powered examples were the result of a direct request from either a regional manager or dealership. Likewise, Six Pack cars could be used as demonstrators and showcase the new engine technology, but the bottom line is that few were loaded up for the simple reason that any serious level of extra equipment pushed the car's retail toward $5,000. Still, a handful received accessories such as power windows and better audio options. Because the base unit was the Road Runner hardtop, the better options available in the GTX line were not available on a Superbird. Incidentally, the optional engine prices on A13s were less than the standard cost of other models; either transmission was the same price.

THE REAL DEAL

As the winter months of 1970 moved toward spring, national sales remained sluggish. Records of teletypes (the printed precursor of email that required a receiving unit for print output) exist showing that some regions failed to sell any 'Birds early in 1970, even after Pete Hamilton's victory at Daytona. Some of the cars were reportedly given to regional sales representatives for company business use as well. The assumption is that this aided in moving cars out of new inventory and into used inventory, where they were sold at far below retail price. By summer, deep discounting programs began to show up around the nation. With a factory retail base price of $4,295, one newspaper advertisement showed prices as low as $3,395 late in the model year.

One ironic outlet, small but visible, was using the cars as pace vehicles at local short tracks. A few cars have seen this as part of their history, including the

Detroit area dealer Ken Brown listed this newspaper-clipped ad sometime late in the year, noting that his price on the final closeout was a mere $3,395. Making 'Birds fly was not easy.

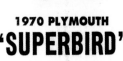

1970 PLYMOUTH 'SUPERBIRD'

IN STOCK! IMMEDIATE DELIVERY! DEMONSTRATION RIDE!

FIRST PLACE WINNER "ALABAMA 500"

LAFLAM-JENTSCH, INC.
Specialist in sales and service of only Plymouth for 15 years.

165 S. BLACK HORSE PIKE
EVE. 'TIL 9 P.M.

RUNNEMEDE 939-1000

1970 PLYMOUTH 'SUPERBIRD'

IN STOCK! IMMEDIATE DELIVERY! DEMONSTRATION RIDE!

FIRST PLACE WINNER "ROCKINGHAM 500"

GARDEN STATE MOTORS
"WORLD'S BEST DEAL"
New Jersey's Largest Imperial Chrysler-Plymouth - Valiant - Simca - Sunbeam Dealer
BLACK HORSE PIKE & ROUTE 130
(1 Mile W. of Kerosites)
WEST COLLINGSWOOD Closed Friday Eves.

UL 4-3230

1970 PLYMOUTH 'SUPERBIRD'

IN STOCK! IMMEDIATE DELIVERY! DEMONSTRATION RIDE!

FIRST PLACE WINNER "DAYTONA 500"

Don Horrow's
WOODBURY CHRYSLER-PLYMOUTH
555 MANTUA AVE., RT. 45
WOODBURY, N. J. 848-6200

The car winning on both ARCA and NASCAR series led to some promotional activities in regional newspapers. This old clipping shows three dealerships in New Jersey showcasing that the cars were winning and now available.

car on this book's cover. Some may have been presented for this use and then written off completely by the supplying dealership as a promotional loss. However, there were no easy solutions to the problems. In some cases, dealerships had the cars somewhere in their inventory into the 1972 model run; a few dealers kept the cars for simple novelty or nostalgia. The final car known to have come off of its factory Manufacturer's States of Origin did so as collectors' interest increased more than a decade later; it sold for the first time in 1985. A more recent example turned up in poorly finished condition. The originating dealer stored the car after his son had an accident with it in 1970.

MARYLAND: THE MUSCLE CAR "KILLER"

Further problems existed relating to some state laws. Maryland's motor vehicles enforcement arm released a statement in April stating that, due to the visual lack of a front bumper, the cars could not be registered in the state. The resolution on this issue is murky. In a 1995 interview with me, corporate employee and

Selling for $140,000 at a Mecum auction in mid-2015, this unrestored U-code 440 version of the A13 package is noteworthy as the final example known to come off of a factory MSO, doing so 15 years after the fact in 1985.

drag racer John Tedder (now deceased) noted vaguely that he had to address this problem for the company and had little success. Rumors suggest that any Superbird returned to a dealer because of this issue ended up reassigned to the used car pool in the southeast, but no proof exists. Moreover, some states required a front plate; factory instructions to dealerships show the process of modifying the nose cone to meet this need.

ROAD RUNNERS REVISITED

In an interview conducted in the 1990s, engineer George Wallace noted the problems with sales had resulted in some cars being converted back into standard Road Runners. This would have been an expensive proposition, because the whole front clip and associated trim would have been needed, as well as body work to the rear quarter panel where the wing had been mounted. It is assumed that the rear window plug would have remained in place, as would any Superbird-related inner bracing and the large hole in the firewall related to operating the vacuum-assisted headlamps.

However, it should be taken into account that this rare occurrence may have also been the result of accidental damage to the vehicle's pointed nose while the dealership owned it. Regardless, it is thought that any such conversions to conventional trim were made well after the model year was complete, and, considering that no more high-compression supercars were available from Chrysler, it is possible that re-equipping a 1970 car with the normalized accessories was attractive enough to justify the expenditure. Again, as with the issue of Maryland's car returns, little is known of this in documentable terms.

SUPERBIRD . . . LESS

Collector Jeff Wickstrom was a young man who bought a Road Runner in the mid-1980s that may or may not have been sold new as a Superbird; but it was certainly built as one. The car is now restored as a standard A13 package, worth more than the novelty value of a modified car. He recalls details of this vehicle after he bought it.

"You can see the chrome window trim on the front and the window plug on the back," he states, referring to a handful of vintage photos that survive. "It also had the 'Bird-specific latch-tray mounting tab welded to the radiator core support. The headlight door vacuum lines [3] were cut off at the firewall but still intact to the headlight switch.

"I never could find any formal documentation/evidence that the dealer did this, and even if I had, I doubt I would have left [the car] that way," he adds. "The earliest image I saw of it was from the previous owner,

Jeff Wickstrom purchased a used Road Runner in the late 1970s that was shorn of its wing and nose; a handful of pictures survive and he later returned it to full Superbird status. He noted that the woman from whom he purchased the car had a photo of it in the modified form from 1972, and was purchased that way. The window and A-pillar chrome trim remained in place. (Photo Courtesy Jeff Wickstrom)

around 1972, with no wing/nose. She wouldn't give me the picture."

Therefore, between being hard to move, easily nose-damaged, sometimes difficult to insure or even register, and, frankly, being a proverbial albatross to some dealerships, the new car market was a challenge for these cars. That said, they rapidly grew in popularity on the collector's market as soon as muscle cars were being preserved as mementos of the era.

OTHER MARKETING EFFORTS

While direct factory marketing was not overt, Superbirds were used at a variety of promotional events, including giveaways. Lowes gave away a code-999 (Corporate Petty Blue) example as part of a 1971 lawn mower promotion with Richard Petty. Champion spark plugs used an image of Pete Hamilton in a black-and-white full-page ad in *Life* magazine. Other automotive firms that used racing imagery for promotion could also have featured the cars in this manner. In general, however, the wing cars were not overly visible following their release.

Although some die-cast models, kits, and toys have appeared in more recent years, the factory is not known to have ever created a promotional model ("promo") of the car. These were colorful plastic replicas that dealers used to show colors to potential buyers; they are highly collectible today. JoHan created the only period models. Using the same molds, it released a Richard Petty #43 NASCAR version as well as the Sox & Martin drag car in 1/24-scale kit format. Unbuilt examples from the first years are pricey today. In recent years, other model companies have created street versions, although most are now out of production.

Best known now in terms of toy reproduction of a Superbird is Strip "The King" Weathers, a cartoon version of the #43 used in the Pixar movie *Cars* in 2006, with Mr. Petty doing the voice-over for the production. A small-scale 1/55 model was released to the general toy market. The trademarked Road Runner visage seen on the Superbird restricts its use on many secondary items, a factor that understandably contributes to the lack of significant marketing of replicas.

Now a national chain, regional hardware store Lowe's promoted a Superbird giveaway with Richard Petty's endorsement during 1970. The car was a 440 model in code 999 Corporate (Petty) Blue and its location today is unknown.

WINGS IN FLIGHT: THE SUPERBIRD IN COMPETITION

The fact that, in mid-1969, Plymouth committed to produce the Superbird is a unique realization of how important racing and victory were to the company. The primary catalyst for building the car was regaining the services of Richard Petty, who had chosen to race a Ford when he had not been offered an aerodynamically competitive Plymouth for 1969. In hindsight, it took a good deal of almost foolhardy optimism by Chrysler to jump forward on this program, but the company saw no other

Richard Petty proudly poses with his Superbird; it is believed that this image was taken at the car's first race appearance, at Riverside in early 1970. (Cal Lane Photo, Courtesy Ray Mann Archive)

Pete Hamilton gets a low-line run on his competition during his winning charge at the 1970 Daytona 500. He followed that up with victories at both 1970 Talladega race events. (Cal Lane Photo, Courtesy Ray Mann Archive)

alternative to resolving the challenge.

I have already described the effort it took to create these cars for production. Considering what that required, it is understandable why a compressed schedule left precious little time to do actual track testing before the 1969 season concluded. Nevertheless, the stylists did not have to rework much to make it a more palatable street package. In addition, the members of the Chrysler engineering group that focused on NASCAR, especially the brilliant George Wallace, were already generating reams of aero and suspension data from the Charger Daytona effort.

Therefore, some baselines were already available for circle track racing, and it was early 1970 before the first real track testing started on the Superbird. In fact, it wasn't until the days leading up to the *Motor Trend* 500 at Riverside, California, in January that Richard Petty had his first chance to drive a beaked 'Bird. The first thing he recognized was the challenge of gauging how long that pointed nose was.

1970 Motor Trend 500

In an interview with Frank Moriarty, author of two books about the era, Petty said that the team's solution was to mount an auto parts–store radio antenna on the point of the nose during qualifying. After getting

a bearing on the length, the antenna was removed for the race, for which Petty and new Plymouth driver Dan Gurney were in Plymouth wings. Nichels Engineering prepped both cars. Chrysler's factory business was not fully under Petty's auspices until 1971.

Petty drove his just-completed team car; Gurney, a seasoned road racer, was in a factory test mule painted as #42 (likely Nichels chassis P37). This was Gurney's only NASCAR event that season, but he took the pole. However, his car suffered brake problems during the

Legendary road racer Dan Gurney and his AAR (All-American Racers) were committed to Plymouth in 1970, and best known for the 'Cuda AAR package in SCCA. With this borrowed Superbird, he ended up on the pole at Riverside, the legendary California racetrack that opened each year of the NASCAR season in that era. It was his only start of the 1970 Grand National season. (Photo Courtesy David Bryant)

race and he finished 6th, right behind Petty's new wing. The highest Plymouth finisher was reigning USAC champion Roger McCluskey, also in his only 1970 NASCAR appearance, who came in 2nd with Norm Nelson's brand-new Nichels #1 Superbird.

Working on Gurney's car that weekend was a new hire, Pete Hamilton, who became the Petty team's second driver for the rest of the season. Hamilton played a significant role in how well the Superbird did in 1970. A former sportsman racer who had won a Grand National touring-class crown, Hamilton came with both a solid New England work ethic and a college-derived understanding of mechanics and mathematics that helped him become good friends with guys at Chrysler Engineering. He was scheduled to campaign an abbreviated 1970 schedule. His first drive for Petty was at the Daytona 500 the following month. Being unknown to the sport's big names and also fearless, he used a bit of psychology to do well at that event.

At the high-speed tracks such as Daytona, drivers were understandably more comfortable with others they already knew, or, as Hamilton told Moriarty, "had a book on." Unabashedly willing to go to the limit on the gas pedal, Hamilton ran Petty's new 7-UP–backed #40 wing faster than he had ever driven before, right from the first

In 1969, Richard Brickhouse won the first race at Talladega in a Dodge. Corporate friends set him up in a Superbird for some 1970 events. This #14 car, owned by Bill Ellis, finished the Daytona 500 in 6th place that weekend. (Cal Lane Photo, Courtesy Ray Mann Archive)

lap. The veteran pilots who questioned his sanity gave him room; he knew this and used it to his advantage to push to the front.

1970 Daytona 500

The race helped launch the single full NASCAR season in which the Dodge and Plymouth aero cars competed. Among those in Superbirds were the two Petty Enterprises entries (Hamilton, #40, and Petty, #43), Dick Brooks in #32, ARCA standout Ramo Stott in #7, and Richard Brickhouse in the Bill Ellis #14. Ironically, the pilot most expected to win, Petty, suffered an engine failure on lap 7, and became a spectator. When it was over, Brooks was 19th following an engine failure, Stott was 8th, Brickhouse came in 6th, and Pete Hamilton won the event. Indeed, Brooks's late race caution gave Pete the chance to get tires, which allowed him to chase down David Pearson, who was leading at the time. Driving flat-out, Hamilton's Superbird gave Plymouth its first Daytona 500 title since 1966.

1970 Carolina 500 and 1970 Atlanta 500

The wings were most effective on the larger banked tracks; their next appearance was at Rockingham, North Carolina, on March 8. Petty won this event to give the 'Bird another feather; Brooks was 3rd and Hamilton was 5th. This trio was also Plymouth's three-aero entry in Atlanta at the end of the month. A Dodge Daytona scored the victory (Bobby Allison), Hamilton was 3rd, Petty was 5th, and Brooks bowed out with an engine problem in 26th place.

1970 Alabama 500

It might seem odd that so few drivers were in the Plymouths, but truth be told, the most visible models for 1970 were the aero 1969 Dodges and Fords; the Daytonas outnumbered the Superbirds at every event that year. However, in racing, you do not need all the cars, just the winner. Pete Hamilton proved that point to be true when he got his first taste of Talladega in

Richard Petty on Driving the Superbird

Richard Petty spoke about the Superbird with Frank Moriarty in Frank's book *Top Speed*. "The problem that we had with that car was getting it turned," noted Petty. "Most cars up to that time, you could turn the car but then the car would get loose and feel so free in the back that maybe you'd have to let off. The problem that we had with the car was that when you'd get to the end of the straightaway you'd be running so fast, you'd turn it, and you had so much overhang in the front that the car wouldn't turn down into the corner. So we spent more time, in fact we spent all year working with that.

"I don't guess we really solved it completely, but by the end of the year we had it down pretty good; and then we didn't get to run them in 1971. We had them big spoilers on the front, and we used to do trick stuff with the spoilers and everything on the front of the car to get the car to turn. The rear, you never had any trouble. You had that wing and you'd just tilt that thing any way you wanted to; and just nail that thing to the ground. It was really an easy car to drive from being comfortable, you could really make it comfortable. The big problem that you had at Charlotte or anywhere else was getting the car to turn.

"It was all but impossible to spin one of them out at speed. You see these cats when they'd blow the motors, or have trouble when they'd blow a tire, and you'd see

Richard Petty at speed during the Daytona 500. Note that there is no window net. (Cal Lane Photo, Courtesy Ray Mann Archive)

these cars get completely sideways and then they'd slide a little bit. But before long the front would come back to the front of the car. I don't know that I've ever seen one completely spin out. I guess they did. When they'd get around there that wind would just catch that rudder on the side and stabilize that thing on up. You see, that's the trouble that they're having with the cars now; once they start off they just go right on around because there's nothing back there to hold them.

"That's the reason they put those deals in the top now, so they'll fly up and keep the car on the ground. If they had those stabilizer deals you wouldn't have that problem."

---

early April. The monster tracks became the young man's forte, and he admitted later that he probably took more chances than the seasoned drivers who had felt the pains of burns or broken bones.

Ramo Stott won the ARCA 125 event in the #7 leading 29 of the 50 laps, but he was not in the field for the Alabama 500 on Sunday, which left the four other 'Birds from Daytona: Petty, Hamilton, Brooks, and the Bill

Ellis machine (driven by Fred Fryer). All finished the race running: Brooks in 13th, Petty in 7th, Fryer scored one lap ahead of him in 6th, and Hamilton again smacking the field down. This time, it was Bobby Isaac in the K&K Insurance Daytona who received the bridesmaid honors. Isaac, who had been the pole sitter, thought he was ahead of Hamilton in the final laps and believed he had won.

Ramo Stott proved to be a serious runner on the ARCA circuit, winning back-to-back titles at Daytona in 1970–1971 in his #7 wing car. Stott, from Iowa, was one of only a couple of drivers in the special cars in the Midwestern-based series. (Cal Lane Photo, Courtesy Ray Mann Archive)

1970 Rebel 400

May's races began at the legendary Darlington Raceway for the Rebel 400. It was here that Dick Brooks came closest to winning a race crown in a wing; he finished 2nd in his #32 Bestline Superbird behind David Pearson. Hamilton was already out due to an engine failure, finishing 19th. However, the big news was Petty's wrecks. Richard wrecked the Superbird during time trials, and, with no aero backup, the team went home and returned with the conventional 1970 Road Runner he had been racing on the shorter tracks.

After admitting that it was not handling well, Petty made history as ABC Sports went live with its mid-race coverage. Soon after, this second car crashed heavily into the concrete pit wall, rolled several times, and ended upside down with Petty unconscious and his now-injured arm hanging out onto the track. This incident, coupled to Hamilton's partial schedule, unfortunately precluded any chance of Plymouth seeing a Petty Superbird win the 1970 Championship.

King Richard was out for several weeks while recovering. It was enough time to help Dodge's Bobby Isaac and crew chief Harry Hyde push toward what became the 1970 Grand National title. Isaac won four of the next five events, all short-track victories.

Dick Brooks had his best Superbird finish at Darlington in the spring, taking 2nd there in the Bestline #32 Plymouth. Brooks would be the final driver to win in a Plymouth three seasons later, and the last driver of a Chrysler aero-model in competition, piloting Mario Rossi's 305-ci Dodge Daytona at the 1971 Daytona 500. (Cal Lane Photo, Courtesy Ray Mann Archive)

1970 World 600

The next big track was Charlotte for the World 600 on Memorial Day weekend. Four Plymouth wings were on hand for the longest event on tour. Jim Paschal was substitute driving the #43, Hamilton was in the #40, Brooks was in the #32, and Bugs Stevens drove the Dick Brown/Bill Ellis #36. Brooks had a crash on lap 127, and Paschal's day ended with overheating issues on lap 325. Hamilton finished in the running 12 laps down, at 8th; Stevens, who ran just three races in his whole Grand National career (all in Superbirds and all in 1970), took home a 6th-place finish.

1970 Motor State 400 and 1970 Falstaff 400

On June 7, Petty was back in action, still on the mend but running in Michigan. Because Brooks's wing car was not yet repaired, only the Petty Superbirds were running there. Petty finished 28th with ignition problems; Hamilton hustled to the 2nd position behind Cale Yarborough's Mercury. However, Petty was in the Winner's Circle on the following Sunday back on Riverside's curves; independent John Soares Jr. and #08 finished 4th; and Dick Bown, in the Mike Ober #02 Superbird, ended 25th after losing a wheel.

Pete Hamilton on Driving the Superbird

In Moriarty's *Top Speed*, Pete Hamilton said, "That was the first time I drove a wing car, at Daytona. I never tested in it. The cars, when you drove them, didn't feel that much different than the 1969 car because even though the speed was 4 or 5 mph faster they didn't feel it. When you run 190, 191, and you run 195, 196, you don't feel that much difference in the speed. We were able to make the car very tight. The back end wouldn't come out; it wouldn't oversteer as much as we were used to.

"The pointed nose, all that did was reduce the amount of horsepower required to run a certain speed. The pointed nose got us down the straightway a little quicker. The vertical stabilizer in the rear, in a neutral position, even without any rake to it, adding 1 or 2 degrees of rake to it really made a big difference. If you left it just as an airfoil, and sprung the car properly, you could leave it flat and you had the least amount of drag for the most amount of downforce in a neutral position. And all of this was unheard of on a stock car, what the engineers call an "overturn couple." It's the percent of downforce on the front versus the percent of downforce on the rear.

"We found a direct set of numbers that was crucial; there was a specific overturn couple that we needed at the big tracks, and another one for 1½ miles, and another one for 1-milers, one for flat tracks, one for the short tracks. We had a set of numbers for the springs; we had a 'roll-couple' relationship with the resistance of roll in the front versus the resistance of roll in the rear. And we had an aero overturn couple that was determined in a wind tunnel.

"The vertical stabilizers were crucial to that car and as the year went on and our testing went on, we did a lot with those stabilizers. When a car would get to a certain degree of yaw, by moving that aero center of pressure to the rear like the sail in a sailboat, you could almost lay it against the wind bank. The more yaw you got into, the more wind bank you had, which would straighten them out like an arrow's feather in the rear, it would help those cars run straight. We tested at Talladega and the engineers would tell us you couldn't spin the car out; that was BS, but you could certainly run a looser car, which was speed. You could throw the car in the corner more."

Pete Hamilton celebrates in the winner's circle, with the only aero-model Chrysler to win a Grand National series event title at Daytona. (Cal Lane Photo, Courtesy Ray Mann Archive)

1970 Firecracker 400

A handful of short-track events led to the July 4 Firecracker 400 in Daytona. Brooks's wing was back in action and Dr. Don Tarr joined him. Tarr normally raced Dodges but was in his only Superbird appearance there. Petty and Hamilton made it four, but Hamilton was out with ignition problems on lap 46 to finish 30th; the #43 again blew an engine, finishing 18th. Brooks and Tarr both finished running a couple of laps down, in 5th and 6th respectively. Amazingly, Dodge was denied a Daytona title yet again when Donnie Allison's Ford led the Charger Daytonas of Buddy Baker and Bobby Allison in a close finish.

1970 Shaefer 300 and 1970 Dixie 500

On July 12, Petty won in New Jersey at Trenton Speedway in the 'Bird; Brooks was 4th. The drivers were finding that the cars worked well on shorter tracks (although the New Jersey facility was a whole 1½ miles) if you could keep the nose out of trouble. Indeed, Dick Bown came east and ran three Tennessee races in Mike Ober's #02 that month: Bristol, Maryville (finishing 6th), and Nashville, the only wing at the latter two. Then it was back to Atlanta on August 2 for the Dixie 500, when Richard Petty took another win in the #43 wing.

August on a Wing

Atlanta was the largest Superbird showing since Daytona, with Petty winning, Hamilton in 6th, Bown in 19th but still running, and Brooks crashing out on lap 219 to finish 26th. Bugs Stevens's #36 was gone first with a blown engine on lap 24. On August 16 at Michigan International, the Chrysler program finally showed the dominance for which it had been created, with Charlie Glotzbach's Charger Daytona both on the pole and in the winner's circle, and wings in places 1 through 6. It was perhaps bittersweet because this event was also the debut of the Hemi-choking restrictor plates. Superbirds finished 3rd (Brooks) and 5th (Hamilton) in this bunch, with Petty 14 laps down in 14th. A week later, Talla-

Collector Todd Werner chased down a Superbird, that was initially restored, believing it to be Pete Hamilton's. Upon additional forensic research and rare photo discoveries, the car has now proven to be the Richard Petty example. Here, Werner is piloting the freshly restored car during an aero-car demonstration at Atlanta Motor Speedway.

dega again roared with power. No less than 15 wings on hand, and Hamilton again showed the way, drafting with Glotzbach's Dodge (a lap down) to save fuel and beating an out-of-gas Bobby Isaac by 10 seconds for his third superspeedway win. A 50-car field, Petty (#43) and Ramo Stott (#77) were 7th and 8th, respectively, to give Plymouth three top-10 spots; Brooks was in 40th with more engine problems. Neither the 38,000 fans on hand nor anyone else that day knew that this would be the final superspeedway event run with competitive aero cars.

Birds into September and Beyond

Richard Petty won the next two short-track events in his conventional car. Labor Day at Darlington on September 7 found Buddy Baker's Dodge winning, with Hamilton in 3rd, Petty in 5th, Brooks in 8th, and Stevens's final Grand National race in 38th with engine damage. On September 20, just one wing was on hand at Dover, Petty's #43, and it went out with a win to score the Superbird's final victory in Grand National racing. Indeed, this was also the final-ever Chrysler aero model event title; Fords won the final two high-bank events at which the cars raced in 1970. The first, the National 500 at Charlotte, was a Plymouth blowout. Both Petty and Hamilton crashed, finishing 23rd and 24th, respectively; Butch Hirst, in the Richard Brown #36, finished 25th.

Due to his short schedule for 1970, we will never know if Pete Hamilton could have coupled his strong winning superspeedway effort to a Grand National title. Regardless, Richard Petty likely would have won that crown except for his devastating May accident. Hamilton drove for Cotton Owens in 1971. (Cal Lane Photo, Courtesy Ray Mann Archive)

Brooks was 30th, again with engine woes.

Although a Texas race was scheduled for December, it was cancelled as the national economy soured, which made the American 500 at Rockingham on November 15 the last aero-competitive race. Yarborough and Pearson gave Mercury and Ford a 1-2 finish to conclude the era, with Petty running 12 laps down in 6th, and Hamilton crashing on lap 449 to finish 15th. Richard Brown's #36, now piloted by Roy Mayne in its final appearance, was in 23rd, and Brooks was gone at 39th of 40 starters, with a blown engine on lap 43. Ironically, Petty's posted winnings for Dover were $1,920. It was almost a symbolic dollar for every Superbird that Plymouth had built to make it possible.

No Crown for the King

Had Richard Petty not been injured at Darlington, it is quite likely that he would have won the 1970 title for Plymouth. In 40 events, he led more than 5,000 laps and won 18 races, compared to actual champion Bobby Isaac, who won 11 events and led 3,188 in 47 showings. This is not to demean Isaac's hard-fought victory, but it simply shows that without adding those missed seven races, Petty had no chance at the crown. He was

4th behind Isaac, Bobby Allison in Rossi's Daytona, and James Hylton's Ford. Still, Petty was 2nd in season-long money at $151,124, and Hamilton, who ran 16 events, was 4th thanks to his huge superspeedway totals, at $131,406. When Bill France announced that there would be a 5-liter (305-ci) restriction on *all* aero models for 1971, the cars were basically rendered non-competitive. Brooks's 7th-place finish in the Rossi Dodge entry at Daytona the following spring closed the era.

WINGS IN OTHER FLIGHT PATTERNS

Although NASCAR's Grand National program was the most visible place for the Superbird to race, it was not the most successful. That honor went to the Midwest USAC circuit, where Norm Nelson and his teammate Roger McCluskey wrestled to take home victory from drivers including A. J. Foyt and Don White. A total of 21 events were scheduled for 1970 at various tracks nationwide.

Wearing #1, McCluskey was USAC's reigning champ and won the season-opener at Sears Point, California, in early April; car owner Nelson finished 3rd in the #41. When completed, this circuit found the two Plymouths

While wings disappeared from NASCAR after the start of 1971, Norm Nelson and Roger McCluskey were among a handful of drivers who raced Superbirds until the cars fell under the two-year-old-body rule in the USAC stock car series. Primarily a Midwestern group, both drivers were successful in Chrysler products during the muscle car era. (Cal Lane Photo, Courtesy Ray Mann Archive)

finishing 1st and 2nd in points; the Nelson/McCluskey duo rotated between one wing and one conventional entry in 1970. Sal Tovella's #37 Plymouth wing and the Ramo Stott–owned #77 Superbird (piloted by Lem Blankenship) joined them to hold up the Plymouth banner.

The biggest event of the USAC season was at the Milwaukee Mile on July 12, where McCluskey won. Wings took five of the top six spots and Chryslers dominated all top-10 positions.

Superbirds in 1971

Even though NASCAR said no more wings for 1971, the 'Birds still flew on the USAC circuit the following season. Nelson purchased the Nichels's shop 'Bird in mid-1971, and the four aero-Plymouth drivers (McCluskey, Nelson, Blankenship, and Tovella) finished in the top five on August 22 for the Fair Stock 200 at the Milwaukee Mile, in West Allis, Wisconsin. When the circuit returned to Milwaukee again for the Governor's Cup 250 in September, six wings chased Al Unser's Ford to the finish line in what may have been USAC's largest ever showing of Detroit's aero specials: five Superbirds, seven Daytonas, and nine Torino Talladegas.

Superbirds were McCluskey in 2nd, Bobby Unser in 3rd in Ray Nichels's shop #10, Nelson in 4th, Blankenship in 7th behind two other Dodge wings, and Sal Tovella in 13th. The 1971 season crown was won by Dodge man Butch Hartman, who ran a Daytona wherever feasible and had excellent finishes all season, including his win while running at Pocono for the first time in September 1971.

1972 Pennsylvania 500

Pocono was a new facility with three different corners, set in the mountains of eastern Pennsylvania. It played the swan song for the wings during the 1972 season. Things had changed radically by then; Petty was winning Grand National races in a Dodge, and a new breed of racing technology using smaller engines was well underway. McCluskey won at Milwaukee yet again

on July 9 in Nelson's wing, now wearing #3, after finishing the 1971 season behind Hartman and Jack Bowsher. And, because his car could no longer run in the ARCA circuit, Ramo Stott raced at Michigan International in his #47 wing the following weekend, where he won. On July 30, a variety of name racers came to Pocono to compete in the only USAC/NASCAR heads-up competition ever held. Richard Petty later noted wistfully that, had it been possible, he would have raced a Superbird there, but wings #40 and #43 had long ago been sold and there were no race-ready replacements.

The race was 200 laps; McCluskey led 180 of them in his wing to finish four laps ahead of the field. The two-year-or-newer rule had already pushed the Daytonas out of competition, so Sal Tovella was 11th, Ramo Stott was 21st (just ahead of Petty's 1972 Dodge, which blew an engine on Lap 118), and Wally Dallenbach in Nelson's #11 wing in 24th. The shocker came in August at Milwaukee when McCluskey failed to qualify. The top wing was Bobby Unser in the Nichels's Superbird, which finished 2nd, with Stott in 6th and Tovella in 33rd due to overheating. Unser never did win with his

Roger McCluskey en route to victory at the event in Pocono that pitted USCA stars against Grand National series heroes including Richard Petty. This should be considered the final big track race of the aero warriors. The 429-ci callout on the hood references the additional bore on the Chrysler Hemi to creep up on the 430-ci USAC displacement limit. (Photo Courtesy Doug Schellinger Collection)

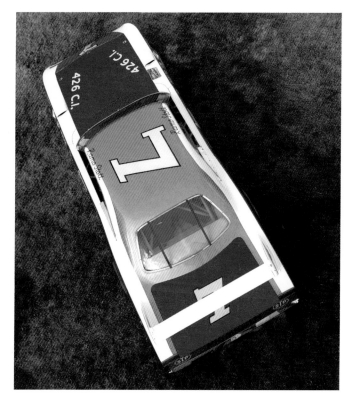

Doug Schellinger, researcher and noted aero-car authority, bought the original Ramo Stott competition Superbird and restored it to its 1970 configuration. The car is seen on the lawn of the Wellborn estate during the 2015 wing car reunion, one of few real race cars that survived to the current day.

Dale Kuehn of Texas put his own spin on Superbird history, creating a car from a standard 383 Road Runner and subsequently running it in legal street course events in the southwest several years ago.

Ramo Stott's #7, the only Superbird to run regularly, dominated the series. In 1970, Stott won the 300-mile ARCA race at Daytona, then a 125-mile preview event at Talladega in April, followed by the actual 500 mile ARCA Vulcan 500 at Talladega on June 14. These, plus six more wins in his standard 1970 Road Runner, easily gave him the crown in the 20-race schedule. The Stott Superbird ended up running primarily with Lem Blankenship on the faster USAC tracks in 1971 except for Ramo's uneventful ARCA appearance at Daytona for Speed Weeks (no Talladega races remained on the ARCA schedule). Stott repeated his Plymouth championship in 1971, and then ran the wings' finale season wherever possible on the USAC circuit in 1972.

Nichels-owned ride, but posted several runner-ups. Hartman, in a 1972 Charger, won the second of his four consecutive championships, with McCluskey in 2nd.

The USAC aero car age ended because of the body rule. Incidentally, USAC remained at a 430-ci limit and without restrictor plates through this entire era. No tracks on that circuit were long enough to make a huge difference in this case.

Ramo's Dominance

ARCA, a series of Midwestern superspeedway races, was in better graces with Bill France than USAC.

DRAGGIN' WINGS AND MORE

The Superbird was created primarily for circle-track action, but Plymouth needed to sell the street models. A handful of Hemi models were notable in drag racing. With Hemi power, the package could fit into Super Stock (SS/E or SS/EA), Stock (C/S or C/SA), and Modified (C/MP). During the 1970 season, a couple of significant examples ended up on the quarter-mile.

Sox & Martin

The Sox & Martin team had debuted a 4-speed

The Sox & Martin Superbird is in the pits at York US-30 Dragway's Super Stock Nationals in 1970. This car has no vinyl top and may have come directly from Petty Enterprises. Its whereabouts are unknown today, but rumors suggest that it was destroyed. (Quarter Milestones Publishing, Pit Slides Archive. All rights reserved)

The SS/EA Karl Gould Hemi Plymouth Superbird was a serious Division 1 player and was tuned and driven by championship Top Fuel tuner Tim Richards. Its big claim to fame was beating the Ray Allen LS6 Chevelle in a match during a late season points race. (Photo Courtesy Mike Hill)

Hemi wing in SS/E that spring, which Joe Fisher, who worked in the Burlington, North Carolina, race shop, had promptly driven into the NHRA record books with a 124.83 speed. The car, likely acquired from Petty Enterprises in nearby Randleman, was raced early in the season without a vinyl top or fender scoops. So the 'Bird was a good fit for the class's NHRA weight-to–factored horsepower (465) index. It just wasn't as good as Ray Allen's automatic Chevy. The Sox shop car was later converted to run in Modified Production with a Six Pack scoop and more liberal changes.

Karl Gould and Tim Richards

Karl Gould, a C-P dealership in Vestal, New York, sponsored the most successful 'Bird, a Hemi automatic, that was owned by Paul Messemer and driven by Tim Richards. Richards was a transmission builder whose nitromethane prowess later pushed Top Fuel racer Joe Amato to record speeds and multiple NHRA championships. The example showed up in late spring and was campaigned for the rest of the season. Richards won the tough SS/EA title at the NHRA Summernationals

and contended for the 1970 Northeast Division 1 Super Stock All-Stars Circuit points all the way to the final event at Raceway Park in Englishtown, New Jersey. He fell to season-winner Bill Morgan's 1970 Hemicuda in the final, but that same day, he beat the LS6 Chevelle fair and square, 11.51 to 11.54. In fact, *Super Stock* magazine editor Jim McCraw specifically noted Richards's effort as part of Plymouth winning its only-ever NHRA manufacturers title that season.

Jack Werst

Perhaps the most notable was the Jack Werst–driven SS/EA Hemi-automatic model, which made just one competitive appearance. Based on weight, SS/EA was the home of Chrysler's Hemi B-Body models that year. Werst worked for Chrysler-Plymouth's Philadelphia zone office, and had tight factory connections. Even though he was racing in Pro Stock already, the catalyst for the car was that a New Jersey team realized that the convertible model of the new 454-ci LS6 Chevelle was also a perfect fit for the SS/EA class. At the advertised 3,837-pound curb weight, the Hemi Superbird factored out to 8.25 pounds per horsepower, and the 454 Chevrolet was an amazing 8.03 (the minimum was 8.00). When Ralph Truppi and Tommy Kling got Ray Allen behind the wheel of the new Briggs Chevrolet entry, it

Thanks to Tom McCrea, there is proof of Jack Werst racing Ray Allen. This is the first round of SS/EA class at Indy in 1970, and Werst later admitted that this car was a big-inch ringer. He got the car back to the hotel before anybody could get a closer look. (Tom McCrea Photo)

The Werst car survives in the paint it wore from the early 1970s when the Tosten & Jennings team owned it. It is on the trailer of its current caretakers at sunset during one of the York US-30 Dragway Reunions.

was a truly dominant combination.

Allen showed that he would be a real threat to the Mopar troops at the upcoming U.S. Nationals in Indianapolis over Labor Day, while Werst's car would become the most well-known non-winning wing in Chrysler history. Werst's car was delivered from Petty Engineering, without the vinyl top and was noted on a Superbird registry of VINs that were slated for circle track work. With a dealer-installed vinyl top and fancy lace paint with Werst's trademark "Mr. 5 & 50" moniker on it, there were several special one-off parts provided that were used to help adjust the weight to the rear. These included lighter front-end pieces, stainless steel and lead-filled C-pillars and panels, .500-inch rear glass, and a weighted wing. Someone at Chrysler also forwarded a 500-ci stroker engine to go under the hood.

It was completely illegal. (Jack later admitted to me that there were disadvantages to being a payrolled Chrysler employee when asked to do such things.) The plan was to try and beat Allen early on, red-light in the following round, and get the car off the property before NHRA found out. The first problem arose when Werst made an evening test run in the sea-level air at Atco, New Jersey, the week prior. He reportedly ran 10.49, which was more in SS/BA territory and, at that time, about 1 second faster than any EA car, ever.

Although Jack's recollection was going rounds in class, research appears to show that the two actually met in round one. Allen deliberately red-lit badly, and Werst did likewise, then drove the Superbird right up on the trailer and left for the motel before anybody asked questions. The tech guys at Indy were very much looking forward to getting a better chance to investigate it. Although NHRA did not use a break rule, after Allen went over to the scales and showed that he was legal, he was reportedly given the default "first or worst" to return for round two. He came back with a vengeance to win the SS/EA class title, which gave him a spot in the final 16-car Super Stock field. In a 1970 Hemi Charger, Dick Landy later lowered the EA record to 11.27 to try and slow Allen down, but, even so, the Chevy won the World Championship. After NHRA reworked the indexes in 1971, all these hijinks were for naught.

Matt Tolbert's *Texas Big Bird* was an IHRA contender in the late 1990s in Pro Modified, long before NHRA recognized the category. Alas, the effort did not produce great victory, and the car ended up in Europe.

Matt Tolbert, Pro Modified

More recently and with much more power, Matt Tolbert ran a Pro Modified Superbird called the *Texas Big Bird* in the IHRA series. He toured for a couple of seasons with little success before the supercharged Hemi creation ended up in Europe. A similar entry was the Graham Ellis twin-turbo Superbird that was both built and raced in England; after posting speeds above 225 mph in the quarter-mile, this machine met with a spectacular demise in 2013 at Santa Pod Raceway.

Jim Frederick's Hemi-powered *Fly Rod* was one of the more visible and active cars on the land-speed circuit, and it hammered out several faster than-200-mph production car record times during its efforts on the salt. (Galen Aasland Photo)

Galen Aasland chose a Max Wedge for his efforts and was rewarded with times that approached the 200-mph mark, including a 198-mph time slip in this 'Bird. (Galen Aasland Photo)

AND THEN ONTO THE SALT . . .

In 1971, reigning Grand National Champion Bobby Isaac made the most noteworthy land-speed effort by any production aero-car in the Harry Hyde–tuned 1969 Dodge Daytona. However, the Plymouth wings also made their marks on the history of land-speed. The most visible of these was likely Jim Frederick, who began an effort that resulted in a record-setting Superbird he called *Fly Rod*. Powered by an injected Hemi engine, the car was classed into B/Altered and set the first of

Pam Beineke on the Road Atlanta road course with the first of the 1971 G-series Superbird II cars that she and her husband Gary built in the 1990s.

many records in 1981 at 211.288. This car was raced on a regular basis from its 1981 debut through 1987.

For those of a more-stock persuasion, the California father/son team of Jim and Larry Lindsley also ran a Superbird. According to Jim's granddaughter, Jim purchased the Alpine White Hemi/automatic for cash

in 1970, took it for a shakedown run at California's El Mirage dry lake, and then made it into a land-speed entry. Storing the OEM parts for future collectability even then, they carefully set the car up and made regular appearances at both El Mirage and Bonneville for the next decade plus; the car eventually topped 221 in

1984 with Larry driving. Daughter Pattie Lindsley Nelson drove it to a 213-mph pass in 1985. Although damaged in a trailer fire coming back from Bonneville that year, the car was repaired and, along with a similar Hemi Superbird (bought as a parts car in the 1970s), was sold to a collector. It remains in the Mopar lobby today.

Other Superbird land-speed efforts include those of Galen Aasland, who ran his entries with normally aspirated 440-ci power. He eventually clocked an incredible 198-mph effort on the salt using a reworked Max Wedge head/intake combination and a 4-speed Mopar A-833 overdrive truck transmission. He still owns this car. Vern Judy also raced a Superbird on the salt, and the legendary Norm Thatcher reportedly had a Superbird that was not raced prior to his untimely death in 1971.

The most recent Superbird worthy of mention was not a 1970 model but rather a 1971. Using the stillborn G-series body changes that were only partially developed before the factory ceased aero development on the 1971 body restyling, noted wing car enthusiasts

Gary and Pam Beineke created two 1971 "what-if" experimental 'Birds. After doing a street version in 2004 with a 472-ci Hemi 6-barrel, painted orange and including options such as the Air Grabber hood, a sunroof, and the never-released John Herlitz–designed Astro-tone dash, they created a second "what-if" for pure speed in 2011. This one is in Corporate Blue (Petty Blue) with a 358-ci R5P7 Dodge NASCAR engine, Jerico transmission (1:1 final ratio), and Moser rear, with #43 graphics. Pam later drove this car to a land-speed record time of 201.6 mph at Loring, Maine.

As mentioned earlier, due to the car's challenging sale issues, a few Superbirds ended up on racetracks, not in competition, but as pace cars. The value of the original cars precludes their use in any arena of competition today, so any restored or verified race-involved example remains treasured by its current caretaker. Almost all of the Superbird race cars, if they had suitable chassis structures by Nichels or others, were rebodied to be conventional Chrysler cars when rules made the design ineligible for racing.

On Atlanta Motor Speedway alongside her husband's what-if #71 Daytona is Pam Beineke in the follow-up #43 land-speed entry. The couple constructed a number of cars based on the canceled G-series Chrysler aero-styling exercises, with this tribute being based on how a 1971 superspeedway Plymouth may have appeared.

There were no Superbird Pro Stock or funny car entries, but Don "The Snake" Prudhomme had help from a fan to tow the 1970 Hot Wheels 'Cuda from the pits to the starting line sometime that fall. (Quarter Milestones Publishing, Pit Slides Series. All rights reserved)

CHAPTER 4

HARDWARE AND FACTORY OPTIONS: WHAT MADE THE 'BIRDS SUPER

This lineup of wing cars at the 2017 Mecum Kissimmee auction featured several colors, options, and all three engine designs.

Detroit produced many unique cars in the muscle car era; however, the Superbird and its predecessor Dodge Charger Daytona were truly in their own league. The required 500 Daytonas were based on converting standard Charger R/T models one by one at Creative Industries; as a result, a sizeable number of the R/T options could be ordered. On the other hand, the assembly-line Plymouth Superbird's unique components and rapid production cycle automatically precluded many potential items on the option form. Moreover, being based on the less-expensive Road Runner design meant that some of the more luxurious appointments available on the Sport Satellite and GTX models could not be ordered on a Superbird. This chapter covers the available optional equipment; further breakdowns are shown in the appendix.

An important caveat to note is that in the constantly fluid reality of assembly-line work, what is noted may have had minor variations. Experts on these cars have seen things that do not seem to match the documenta-tion or the protocols. Therefore, forensic examination is a part of verifying a Superbird's authenticity.

As an example, it is possible that a dealership, trying desperately to get a Superbird off the lot, may have been willing to replace a black vinyl top with a custom-cut white top, or potentially repainting a car to a buying customer's desire. It was sold that way but changes were never reflected in the construction data or broadcast sheets. Adding other factory equipment may have also been possible at the dealership level, and may or may not have been listed on a retail sales form for a new car. However, the changes would not be on its factory-applied Monroney label. In Chrysler vehicle provenance, one thing I have learned is that there are exceptions to every rule.

With that disclaimer made, this map explains what should and should not be present. Let's start with the basics.

Superbirds were part of the Road Runner line, and as such did not have the number of options that the GTX and Sport Satellite designs received.

GENERAL SPECIFICATIONS

Construction, all units	Lynch Road Assembly Plant
Structural Frame	Unitized sub-components
Overall Length (inches)	221.0 (nose to back bumper)
Overall Width (inches)	76.4
Overall Height (inches)	61.4
Wheelbase (inches)	115.8 (standard Plymouth B-Body)
Tread, Front (inches)	59.7
Tread, Rear (inches)	58.7
Fuel Tank Capacity (gallons)	19

The unmistakable look of the Plymouth Superbird from behind featured the high deck wing and, in most cases, chrome tips. This is a restoration of the car that land-speed racer Jim Frederick used on the street; it features white Plymouth lettering on an EK2 Orange body.

Ground Clearance (inches)	7.2
Deck Lid to Wing Height (inches)	24
Weight Balance, Front/ Rear (percent)	54/46
Shipping Weight (pounds)	3,785

A13 SUPERBIRD PACKAGE, STANDARD EQUIPMENT

All A13 builds were considered Special Order (Y39) cars

Engine	440 Super Commando 375-hp, 4-barrel Carter AVS carb
Transmission	A727 3-speed automatic
Differential	8-¾ 3.55 Sure-Grip (A36 Performance Axle Package)
Interior	Black or white vinyl (black headliner only)
Exterior	One of seven designated colors, three Hi-Impact, V19 black vinyl top mandatory
Visual Superbird Component Package	Aero nose cone, front spoiler, front valance, adopted 1970 Coronet fenders, Fury front marker lamps, rear-facing front fender scoops, modified 1970 Coronet hood stamping, chrome hood pins, chrome A-pillar aero trim, special rear window steel plug, special rear window glass, three-part rear wing (uprights and adjustable aluminum horizontal spoiler) with associated hardware, also non-visible subassembly adaptations on body to facilitate all the above, secondary body jack to assist front tire changes, specialty Superbird-only graphics package, and J45 Hood pins

A13 STANDARD SUPERBIRD SUSPENSION PACKAGE

Power steering, power front disc brakes, F70x14 Goodyear WSW (white sidewall) tires, Performance Axle package A33 or A36.

Regardless of which engine and transmission were selected, the Superbird could easily blaze the tires, as owner Tony D'Agostino is aptly demonstrating.

This U-code 440 (375 hp) engine is unrestored and is in an unrestored car. The basic engine was rated at 375 hp and featured a round, dual snorkel air cleaner. A majority of Superbirds used this engine, which was not available in any standard Road Runner model.

The V-code 440 6-barrel (390 hp). The first optional engine added heavy-duty internals and 3x3 Holley carbs. Because of multiple carburetion, this engine used the wide oval air cleaner developed for the Air Grabber package, which was not available on the Superbird.

MANUFACTURER'S SUGGESTED RETAIL PRICE

Base model $4,298.

DRIVELINE OPTIONS

Three engines and two transmission/axle packages could be ordered/installed in a Superbird. There was an upcharge for engine selection but transmission choice was no additional cost. The Superbird was the only 1968–1970 version of the Road Runner to use the A134 440 4-barrel Super Commando engine. It was also the only version of the car from those years not available with any form of the 383-ci engine. The code E86 for the A134 was not on the normal Road Runner option list and was only available as part of the A13 Superbird package.

ENGINE

U-Code Standard

E86	440-ci 4-barrel Super Commando V-8 wedge engine, 375 hp at 4,600, 480 ft-lbs of torque at 3,200, RB block 4.32 x 3.75, 9.7:1 compression, cast-iron heads, cast-iron intake and exhaust manifolds, Carter AVS 4-barrel x 1 carb (carb number varies based on driveline and emissions standards), hydraulic high-lift cam, single-breaker aluminum distributor

This R-code 426 8-barrel (425 hp) was the top engine in the Chrysler arsenal. The NASCAR-developed 426 Hemi used dual Carter AFBs and a new oval air cleaner replaced the former "chrome dome" of previous Hemi releases. It may or may not have a broad Hemi decal on it, as both ways are correct for 1970.

V-Code Six Pack

E87 + $249.55	440-ci 6-barrel V-8 wedge engine, 390 hp at 4,700, 480 ft-lbs of torque at 3,200, RB block 4.32 x 3.75, 10.5:1 compression, cast-iron heads, cast-iron exhaust manifolds, aluminum or cast-iron high-rise intake, Holley 2-barrel x 3 carbs, hydraulic high-lift cam, dual-breaker cast-iron distributor

R-Code Hemi

E74 + S841.05	426-ci Hemi 8-barrel V-8 hemispherical engine, 425 hp at 4,700, 490 ft-lbs of torque at 4,000, RB Hemi block 4.25 x 3.75, 10.25:1 compression, cast-iron heads, cast-iron exhaust manifolds, aluminum high-rise intake, Carter AFB 4-barrel x 2 carbs, hydraulic high-lift cam, dual-breaker cast-iron distributor

TRANSMISSION

D32 w/ A36	Standard equipment A727 TorqueFlite 3-speed automatic, integral B/RB engine bolt pattern
D21 w/ A33	A-833 New Process 4-speed, standard construction, 1970 design

AXLE

052/D56/ D91	Chrysler 8¾-inch design, 3.55:1 ratio, automatic, Sure-Grip (A36 standard)
083/D56/ D91	Dana 60 9¾-inch design, 3.54:1 ratio, manual, Sure-Grip (w/A33)

All Superbirds came with power steering and power front disc brakes, mandating this booster-assist master cylinder. Also seen here are the firewall grommet and vacuum lines to operate the headlamps.

This is a standard Dana 60 differential in an unrestored 440 6-barrel Superbird, whose careful storage and southwestern U.S. ownership preserved much of its assembly-line detail.

EXTERIOR COLOR OPTIONS

The need for subassembly paint applications limited the Superbird in terms of color selection. The first six were in the introductory literature dated October 27, 1969. Code 999 was offered later only to facilitate cars in Petty's Corporate Blue. Therefore, there are seven options; three of these were Hi-Impact (HIP) colors that carried a premium price of $14.05 more than the normal paint. It is documented that a very few Superbirds were painted in FK5 Deep Burnt Orange Metallic; it is quite possible these were miskeyed by striking K instead of J on the keyboard during the initial ordering process. If not caught prior to being moved to the Trim Line, adjustments were made to complete these cars in this unauthorized color by sending additional paint with the car to Clairpointe Street.

Due to time constraints on the program and pre-painted components on hand, it is believed that any special order from an outside source for this or any other unlisted color was immediately denied. Because the package mandated the vinyl roof, all Superbirds are also V01 coded for monotone paint.

EB5	Blue Fire Metallic
EK2	Vitamin "C" Orange (HIP)
EW1	Alpine White
EV2	Tor-Red
FJ5	Lime Light Green (HIP)
FY1	Lemon Twist Yellow (HIP)
999	Corporate (Petty) Blue
FK5	Deep Burnt Orange Metallic (factory error)

INTERIOR COLOR AND TRIM OPTIONS

Only two interior colors, black or white, were offered, and base codes are used for either bench or bucket designs in those tones. Components could be further upgraded based on optionally available Road Runner interior equipment, which did not allow for leather accents. Therefore, there are four interior option codes.

H2X9	Black vinyl bench seating
P6XA	Black vinyl bucket seating
H2XW	White vinyl bench seating
P6XW	White vinyl bucket seating

A look at an unrestored 440 4-barrel Superbird in the Wellborn Musclecar Museum shows that the painter neglected to spray the firewall as this car was being built, leaving the lower area in primer gray only.

The H2X9 black vinyl bench seating in a car that received an AM radio and N95 clock-tach option.

The H2XW white vinyl bench seating in a car that was radio delete and had a non-functional pod where the tach or clock could have been installed.

Superbirds could only be ordered in two interior paint colors, black or white, and was limited to two options as well.

TX9	Black upper body interior paint
EW1	White upper body interior paint

Plymouth Graphics

At Clairpointe Street, the Road Runner/Superbird decals were added as were the large-letter Plymouth decals. These were either white or black, and decal color was predicated on car color; this is not coded anywhere but is charted below for convenience with the paint information in this section. Thanks to David Patik of Performance Car Graphix for this breakdown.

Black Plymouth Decal

EK2	Vitamin "C" Orange (HIP)
EW1	Alpine White
FY1	Lemon Twist Yellow (HIP)
FJ5	Lime Light Green (HIP), most original cars

EK2 Vitamin "C" Orange used a black decal. It is not known why the colors were selected for the offered colors and the documentation on this has been done primarily using existing car research.

EV2 Tor-Red used a white decal. The large Plymouth decal was part of the marketing edge for the company in the racing environment, as if the extra components did not draw enough attention.

White Plymouth Decal

EB5	Blue Fire Metallic
EV2	Tor-Red
FJ5	Lime Light Green (HIP) rarely on original
999	Corporate (Petty) Blue
FK5	Deep Burnt Orange Metallic (factory error)

Obviously, the wrong color could be applied, but FJ5 is the only one believed to have been equipped correctly with either version and may have been so during restoration, based on vehicle demands at Clairpointe Street.

OPTIONAL EQUIPMENT NOT AVAILABLE

A01	Light package
A04	Basic group (already included in A13)
A31/A32/ A34	Performance axle packages (lower-gear ratios)
A35	Trailer towing package
D91	Sure-Grip (already included in A33/A36 axle package)
F25	70-amp battery (included as standard and not to be ordered again)
H31	Rear defroster
H51	Air conditioning
L42	Headlamp delay
M25	Sill molding
N96	Air Grabber
R31	Rear speaker
V21	Hood paint

STANDARD A13 EQUIPMENT NOT NOTED ABOVE

On Superbird fender tags, the following codes should always be present. These were related to mandatory body equipment, delete, and cooling.

V19	Special-order Black vinyl top (coded as standard V1X on some early cars)
V-88	Transverse stripe delete (Road Runner standard "dust trail" for 1970)
26	26-inch radiator (all Superbirds used this unit)

RUNNING PRODUCTION CHANGES

The only noted change made during production of the Superbird specific to this model was the changeover to a non-viscous drive fan to facilitate cooling. Starting on November 5, automatic models using either the E86 or E87 440-ci engines were equipped with a heavy-duty fan and accompanying spacer; this was noted in a Product Information Bulletin to all dealers dated November 25, 1969.

FACTORY OPTIONAL EQUIPMENT LIST

Due to the challenge of getting the Superbirds built on time, the factory worked quickly to construct them. As noted previously, most were sales bank cars and basically optioned to keep the prices low enough to attract sales. Listed are options that could be ordered.

Wheels and Tires

Critical components on a performance car were wheels and tires. Three tires and five wheels were available, with T86 and 17 as standard on 440, U84 and 28 standard on Hemi. The tire size ordered determined

Although a 14-inch whitewall was the base tire, most Superbirds came with these Goodyear Polyglas F70-14 tires. This car has the base code 17 body-color rims.

The top factory tire was the Goodyear Polyglas GT F60-15, shown here on the optional W21 15-inch Rallye wheel.

The spare tire was mounted on a TX9 black-painted rim if the car received Rallye wheels or body color if the car came with the standard rim and small hubcaps; this is a code 28 15-inch version.

This unique plate was installed in the trunk to hold the special frame jack for the front. (Photo Courtesy Ricks)

standard steel wheel size, W codes indicated premium designs (see the broadcast sheet decoder lines 4 and 11 for a further breakdown).

Tires

T86	F70-14 White sidewall, standard
T87	F70-14 Raised white-letter Polyglas
U84	F60-15 Raised white-letter Polyglas GT

Wheels

17	14x6 steel PN3420978 standard w/ 14-inch tires T86/T87
28	15x7 steel wheel PN2944450 standard w/ 15-inch tires U84
W21/61	14x5.5 Rallye
W23/63	14x5.5 five-spoke road wheel (Magnum 500)
W21/71	15x7 Rallye

Spare Wheels
14x6 PN3420978
15x7 PN2944450

Wheel Covers*

W11	14-inch deluxe (full) Plymouth wheel covers
W15	14-inch wire wheel cover PN2944400

Hubcaps; small-diameter version standard

Here is the jack and its components installed on the plate. Note the wing support behind it.

An original spare as installed on the assembly line is shown here; the standard jack was held in place with it. The rim is a code 17 TX9 version because the car received Rallye wheels.

Car Jacks

The Superbird models had two jacks, a standard bumper jack for the rear, placed beneath the full-size spare similar to other B-Body Plymouths, and a special scissor jack for use under the frame to facilitate front wheel changes. This was mounted in the passenger-side rear quarter panel near the rear wheelhouse; the same area had the extra wing supports as well. This jack was held in place by an exclusive-to-Superbird triangular plate attached to a stud assembly welded to the trunk floor.

N-Code Possible or Mandated Engine Accessories

Due to the performance nature of all Superbird models, certain items were coded due to engine design.

N41	Dual exhaust (all Superbirds)
N42	Chrome exhaust tips
N65	Torque-drive fan (all Superbirds; also with non–Torque-drive 440/440-6 and automatic after November 5)
N51	Maximum cooling package (all Superbirds)
N85	Tachometer (note that all N85s are Tic Toc Tach design)
N88	Auto Speed Control, 440 4-barrel only
N95	Evaporative Emissions Control (California-delivered vehicles)

Dual exhaust was installed on all Superbirds. The chrome tips were not mandated, but few cars came without them.

A look at the N85 Tick Tock Tach, Chrysler's combination clock/tachometer offered under N85. Note the brake light indicator and headlight toggle shown here.

INTERIOR OPTIONS

The fact that Superbirds were constructed from base Road Runners precluded some of the better interior amenities that could be found on the GTX. This included power and leather seat options, some dress-up items, and more. Coupled to the reality of the high base price and lack of pre-orders meant that Superbirds were often pretty basic inside. Premiums for consoles and floor shifts were the most important consideration when looking a car for purchase.

Steering Wheel

Popular upgrades for muscle cars were steering wheels. Three were offered, each with a specific center cap exclusive for Road Runner.

The standard steering wheel was coded S79. The 4-speed Pistol Grip is visible behind it; few cars seem to have been optioned with the 4-speed console combination.

59

The deluxe wheel is the S81 three-spoke version with center cap. An S83 Rim-Blow model shows up on the sales paperwork for Belvedere but is not known to have come on these cars.

S79	Standard partial ring wheel w/ code 43 partial ring pad
S83	Rim-Blow two-spoke wheel w/ code 1 rim switch pad
S81	Woodgrain sport three-spoke wheel w/ code 47 center cap pad

Group Packages

Although it is possible that some auxiliary packages could have been ordered on the base Belvedere, none are documented to exist on a Superbird.

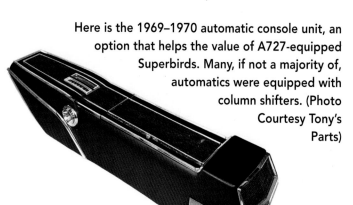

Here is the 1969–1970 automatic console unit, an option that helps the value of A727-equipped Superbirds. Many, if not a majority of, automatics were equipped with column shifters. (Photo Courtesy Tony's Parts)

Console, Floor, Seat Belts

C13	Front shoulder belts, driver and passenger
C14	Rear shoulder belts, driver and passenger
C15	Deluxe belt option: buckle dress-up, warning lamps, brackets
C16	Center console
C21	Center cushion/armrest (buddy seat; no console)
C23	Armrest w/ ashtray
C51	Bench seat split 50/50
C55	Bucket seats
C62	Driver bucket six-way adjustable
C65	Bench seat air foam
C81	Heavy-duty front seat
C83	Heavy-duty rear seat
C85	Heavy-duty both seats
C93	Carpeting
C92	Mats, heavy-duty front and rear, black

Heavy Duty

To date, it is not believed that any Superbird was ordered with fleet equipment for pace car usage when new, some items were available on standard Belvederes and therefore applicable to Road Runner.

F17	Radio suppression package
F25	Mopar heavy-duty 70 amp series 27 battery, black w/ red caps (all Superbirds)
F56	Extreme cold antifreeze treatment (Y07 cars to Canada)
F95	Calibrated speedometer
F96	Oil pressure gauge in dash

Glass Mirrors

G11	Solex-tinted all windows, clear backlight on all Superbirds
G15	Solex-tinted windshield only
G31	Manual passenger outside mirror chrome
G33	Standard driver-side outside mirror chrome
G36	Remote driver-side mirror w/ passenger-side standard mirror
G41	Prismatic rearview mirror
G42	Standard rearview mirror

Heater

H11	Heater front (no rear heat vent or defroster available on Superbird due to back glass change)

Miscellaneous Items

J21	Clock in dash (N/A w/ N95 tach-clock)
J42	Hurst Pistol Grip (all 4-speed cars)
J45	Hood pins (all Superbirds)
J46	Locking gas cap
J55	Undercoating, hood insulation

J45 hood pins were used on all Superbirds. Note the thin plastic snap-in retainer that kept the vacuum lines and wiring together as they traversed the core support to the nose cone.

Lighting and Switches

L65	Ignition switch time delay light
L73	Seat belt unfastened indicator
L75	Warning light low fuel
L76	Heater panel light (standard on all B-Bodies in 1970)

Moldings and Exterior Trim

M05	Chrome door-edge moldings
M26	Wheel lip moldings
M81	Front bumper guards (denotes the rubber and steel nose strip on all Superbirds)
M83	Rear bumper guards
M95	Assist handles over doors

Power Accessory Items

All Superbirds were coded for M81 front bumper guards; this code actually referenced the rubber strip inserted across the cone's leading edge.

Deluxe items including power seats and leather seat accents were not available on Road Runners in 1970, leaving few items in this category. P41 and P45 have not been documented on any Superbird (although they could be ordered on any Belvedere in 1970).

P31	Power windows
P41	Power door locks
P45	Power deck lid

Radio, Antenna, Speakers

Another popular upgrade to add dealer value to the bottom line was radio equipment. Four units were available, two AM versions, an AM/FM version, and an AM/eight-track version. There were no AM/FM/eight-track or cassette units from Chrysler in the 1970 Superbird era.

R11	AM
R13	AM heavy-duty 5.5 watts
R21	AM/FM stereo
R22	AM stereo/eight-track player

Suspension Accessories

All Superbirds came standard with the following suspension equipment:

S15	Extra-heavy-duty Hemi
S25	1-inch heavy-duty front/rear
S31	Front sway bar
S77	Power steering

Export and Canada Codes

X21	240-km speedometer
X25	Driver-side headlamp beam shift
X53	Sealed speedometer
X66	Label for export

A FEW FINAL NOTES ON QUICKLY IDENTIFYING A SUPERBIRD

The following points help identify the remains of a Superbird that might be so decrepit that little remains of its origins.

- RM23U0A (VIN dash, door federal tag, fender tag, paperwork): A majority of these cars were built as 440 Super Commando powered. RM23U is a Superbird-only code. Obviously, if no dash, fender tag, and door tag remain, there is little more that could be used to build the car around, but other fingerprints may exist. Other VIN codes are RM23V0A and RM23ROA.
- Rear window plug: This was the most crucial item on the rebuild, and barring a vehicle being stripped down so severely that it is gone, the plug shows the original Road Runner rear glass stamping directly behind the plug's more streamlined display.
- Rear wing support: There should be welded supports for mounting the wing inside beneath the rear quarter panels.
- Scissor jack stud: The stud for the scissor jack and

mount is welded to the floor near the passenger-side wing support.
- No rear speaker/defroster (package tray): No sign of any speaker or defrost unit mounted in the package tray area. However, at least one car is documented to have received the rear speaker.
- A hole in the firewall for vacuum hoses to operate the headlamp covers: This had a large grommet around it, and even in reputed cases where the nose was changed out by a dealer, it is likely the remains of the vacuum lines were there as well.

The chrome A-pillar trim is rarely seen flat, because the thin steel dimpled during installation.

- 440 to Six Pack change: In some instances, unscrupulous people have attempted to pass off U-code 440 models for the rarer V-code Six Pack examples. These were restored cars with questionable supporting paperwork and freshly recreated faux VIN and fender tags. (It sounds extreme, but this swap is much easier to do than converting a 440 to a Hemi version.) Obviously, check with someone familiar with these cars if there are questions regarding provenance before considering a purchase, and walk away if you remain unconvinced.

Of course, the Road Runner beep-beep horn helped the legacy of the Superbird as well.

Styling for the masses lives on more than 40 years after the cars showed at Talladega to win at both 1970 events thanks to Pete Hamilton, Petty Enterprises, and Plymouth.

CHAPTER 5

A 'BIRD IN HAND: BUYING, COLLECTING, AND RESTORING SUPERBIRDS

With the right optional equipment, in this case EV2 paint and Hemi power, prices on Superbirds have soared into the highest levels of classic-era American supercar collecting. The bid climbed to more than $500,000 during spirited action at Mecum's Kissimmee event in January 2017.

Because you have this book, you probably have more than a passing interest in Plymouth Superbirds. As noted in previous chapters, these cars were not simply unique in appearance but also in construction, street design, and optional equipment. Although new-car dealers may have found them a source of frustration during their release, these special Road Runners have climbed toward much more popularity in the ensuing decades. Today, Superbirds rank among the top echelon of collectible American muscle cars, and examples priced reasonably at the present market demand don't remain unsold for long. Therefore, this conclusion about buying Superbirds or returning them to as-built condition brings this narrative full-circle.

Of the nearly 2,000 or so cars originally created, survival rates may be higher compared to many other models due to their unique appearance. That noted, it is still likely that no more than a third, or approximately 600 to 700 examples, exist today. The easily damaged, hard-to-park long nose, the gas crisis, abuse from poor secondary ownership, and quite frankly, the quickly outlived novelty helped speed up their demise. Conversely, they quickly became favorites of Mopar performance enthusiasts as well as era-specific collectors. The interest in muscle cars grew as their investment stature also grew. As a direct result, there were Superbirds being purchased for that reason even in the mid-1970s. Meanwhile, events including the Mopar Nationals and a

varety of aero-car club meets began to draw further understanding as well as networking by the mid-1980s.

Currently, Superbirds have settled into perhaps the top 10 percent of American collector vehicles from this time period. Examples have sold in excess of a half-million dollars during the past decade, and very few, if any, Hemi-built models are considered unrestorable today. Pricing at these levels can be mercurial. However, should you have the wherewithal to purchase a Superbird today, I can offer you some important advice as you proceed.

The art of collector car restoration has never been better. Today, you see cars that are so meticulous in fitment and finish that they no longer resemble assembly-line construction. In all truthfulness, at the level of value these cars hold, this is not considered

Once upon a time, indeed! The son of the Plymouth dealership's owner went joyriding and partially wrecked this then-new 'Bird. Written off as a complete loss, it was hidden away for a long time and became a true barn find almost a half century later. This was its public reappearance at the 2016 Muscle Car and Corvette Nationals (MCACN).

Evident in this image of an unrepainted wing are signs of pigment fading, the result of using lacquer-based paints during the final process at Clairpointe Street. This is one reason so many Superbirds were repainted early on in their existence.

The interior of the same car, which is unrestored, shows the remarkable condition of the original instrument panel. To the person who desires original cars, this and associated provenance can become very important.

a problem for an owner who desires something truly perfect, even if it represents a better reality than any Superbird showed when new. These cars are done beautifully but embody only a portion of the marketplace.

LEVELS OF COLLECTOR CARS

Other levels beyond absolute perfection for top-value cars are survivors, cars that have been kept in as-built shape, even if showing some signs of wear, and exacting factory-correct restorations that show some of the assembly-line flaws but are otherwise true to stock. The second tier is the most common today, regular-grade often-older restorations showing completeness but not perfection. A third tier is modified or in-process cars that require work to complete or bring back to original, and the final level is damaged or incomplete cars needing full restoration.

Survivor Cars

One of the thriving parts of the current hobby is low-mileage unrestored cars, which feature little or no signs of use, rock-solid provenance, all the proper date-coded parts, primarily unrestored finishes, and verifiable ownership history. The adage that "It can be restored over and over, but is only original once," has become much more prevalent in the car collecting mindset in recent decades. As a result, the best restoration shops now take cars found in this stature to simply blueprint, or precisely detail, them. This may include carefully cleaning, very mild refinishing, and original-only parts upgrading. Such a car retains literally all facets of being original as a result. Refreshing of the lacquer-painted

components on Superbirds that have faded or aged poorly is the one common and often only acceptable compromise for the sake of overall appearance.

Restored Cars

I noted the perfect and assembly-line-correct restorations above. Stepping away from those over-the-top restorations and cars that meet the modern definition of original, you begin to find a broader base of potential investment cars. Older or less-than-complete full restorations often top this category. These are vehicles that showcase overall expert refinishing but may not have been rebuilt with properly dated parts or feature less-exact but OEM-correct replacement drivelines. A majority of post-1990 restorations with minimal added use fit into this category. Remember that exterior enamel finishes that most closely mirror factory construction are never perfect. This exactitude is actually of greater importance to some collectors than mere perfection.

A number of professional-level shops focus solely on Chrysler products. Ken Mosier and his Finer Details business expertly completed this Superbird for Davis Soruk in time to display it at the 2016 MCACN show.

This low-mileage Superbird showed some fading on its lacquer components when collector Tony D'Agostino owned it. Still unrestored, current owner Ryan Clough later had only the nose and fender scoops professionally repainted. The unavoidable pigment wear on these parts was visible under close inspection.

Amateur Restorations

Stepping further away from these higher levels are complete cars that were amateurishly redone, show serious use or abuse, or were modified beyond paint in terms of factory appearance. Some may have major driveline changes or difficult-to-reverse suspension modifications. Because there are varying levels of these changes, it behooves the buyer to determine what the car's true final value might be prior to purchase. A car with customized paint is going to be easier to bring back to stock than a model featuring wheel tubs and traction-enhancing rear suspension changes. Frankly, modified cars of this nature should be only purchased based on the personal tastes of the buyer. In severe instances, after taking the initial purchase cost into consideration, the expenses for a restoration back to stock could outweigh the car's dollar value, so spend wisely.

Basket Cases

The final group of cars are those heavily wrecked, rusted,

Riding on the trailer entering Talladega, Mike Hill found the old Tim Richards's Karl Gould drag car mentioned in chapter 3. It was repainted in the 1970s with amazing murals and colors, presenting a real challenge on the decision to restore this factory E74 Hemi car to OEM status, to as-raced in 1970 paint, or leave as a time capsule in its current 1970s survivor condition. Even though the engine is unfortunately long gone, it is both an incredibly rare car and a unique conversation piece.

Chris Wright's Superbird shows what might have been if the factory had offered a special hood. This was the bulge used on the 1970 Super Bee. Again, these are simple changes that could be reversed if the car were brought back to OEM specifications.

disassembled, or even incomplete accumulations of specialized A13 parts. These cars are those found in such a dilapidated condition that they must forgo the claim of original. They are also cars discovered very incomplete, partially done restorations, bare shells, or vehicle-specific identifiable parts for a project. The latter may be multiple components with matched VIN and fender tag parts for a rebody effort. All of this brings me to the next point. In the end, excepting Hemi examples, many such cars must be judged primarily as their combined parts value, not as vehicles, because so much expense may be required to make them presentable as investment vehicles.

PROVENANCE MATTERS . . . A LOT

One thing that is critical to the investment value of a collector car today is its provenance. Although not spoken about openly, values at this level can lead to less-than-honest duplicating techniques, falsified stampings, and bogus restorations on lesser-value original vehicles. The most critical

removable physical components on the car are the VIN and fender tags; either of these items being absent is problematic as an investment. Of course, both items are simply metal and can be duplicated with some effort.

The issue of rebodying, where a complete donor shell is used to restore a car, is an ongoing challenge. The areas to look for in those cases will likely require you to have access to another real Superbird for comparison. Body serial-number stampings will be found on the sheet metal as well; having experts examine a car of questionable pedigree is always a wise decision. Or, run away . . .

Broadcast Sheet

Having a broadcast sheet related to the car's construction is important as well, even though it's not as critical as the attached metal items noted above. As stated in chapter 3, this paperwork was only released during the car's assembly at Lynch Road, by chance. It was not mandatory, and examples may have been left in various places. I know of one Superbird that yielded four broadcast sheets when disassembled. Even a partial sheet is valued when ascertaining a car's options, and it is the first thing most people look for when taking a car apart. Breaking down the sheet is the roadmap to verify the car's as-built options for both documentation and restoration (see the appendix).

Paperwork and More Paperwork!

Additional provenance includes sales documents of any kind, repair and maintenance records, provable or notarized ownership history, and associated photographic evidence. The latter even pertains to photo documentation of prior restorations. In the end, you are paying for a thoroughbred collectible; the more it lives up to its pedigree, the more it will be valued. I know of an original Superbird's paperwork selling by itself for $1,000 to the new owner. If the car has provenance, be sure you get that when paying and be cautious if someone else possesses that documentation (caveat emptor).

OPTIONS ADD UP

Purchasing any collector car requires that you either desire it or recognize its worth. On muscle cars such as Superbirds, optional equipment correlates directly to value.

Here's an amazing low-mileage Arizona Superbird that was unmolested other than a single older repaint. This was during Vintage Certification evaluation at the 2016 MCACN show.

The broadcast sheet for the Arizona car was used to double-check components such as the propeller (or driveshaft). Thanks to very limited use, and never in poor weather, this car featured many unique and rarely seen details.

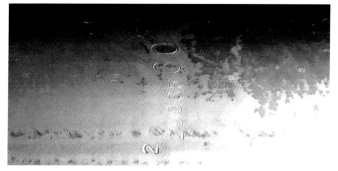

Here is the corresponding number on the shaft. This car was so original that stampings such as this were still extant on one tailpipe, and the factory paper tag was still hooked to the gas tank!

426 Hemi

At the top of this grouping are the more expensive items, of course led by the R-code 426 Hemi engine.

Another Superbird from Mecum Kissimmee that pushed to more than a quarter-million dollars in bids was this unrestored V-code (Six Pack) example optioned with code 999 Corporate (Petty) Blue paint, a 4-speed, and a rare white interior.

This option alone is worth an estimated 75 to 100 percent or more than a base 440 model. The 440 6-barrel V-code would add 15 to 30 percent more than the base model, so the engine choice is a big consideration. This also relates to that engine being the version the car left the factory with, as correct replacement engines are common but never as attractive as the factory-installed example.

Beyond horsepower notoriety, engine value is based on rarity as well. The base U-code was installed in approximately 60 percent of the cars, 1,084 units. About 30 percent, or 716, were V-code models, and less than 10 percent, only 135 cars, came new with the R-code Hemi. Although equal in rarity to the Hemi Daytona Charger, the Dodge commands a premium because of its 503-unit overall production run and availability of better R/T equipment.

The car from Arizona shown previously did not receive undercoating when new. As a result, the correct overspray pattern from the rocker area toward the underside of the car could be seen on the floorpan.

Another image of this car shows some of the correct Dana 60 paint markings from the factory. Details such as this help make unrestored cars so valuable when you know the proper appearance of factory components.

4-Speed w/ Console

The second most important option is transmission and associated shift mechanisms. Because there was no charge added for an A-833 4-speed (normally a less-expensive option than the A13 standard-equipment A727 automatic), cars so equipped are often worth a premium due to the Pistol Grip shifter, Dana differential, and accompanying ideas of performance; optimally it is console-mounted. Factory 4-speed console combinations are not common in Superbirds.

Next is a floor-shift A727 automatic; unlike the stick, this required a center console and associated bucket seats.

The final and standard design was the column shifter, which is most common but unfortunately can be a drag on value even with a Hemi. It does not detract from overall worth of the Superbird package, but the driveline and shifter position is a factor in investment purchase decisions.

Factory Options

The third factor regarding options is other factory-added equipment. Except for the noted components not available on A13 cars, many of the dress-up items available on other Road Runner hardtops could be ordered. This is led by the performance parts (15-inch Polyglas GT tires, 14-inch Polyglas tires, Rallye and road wheels, N95 tachometer, and the C16 console bucket layout).

Next are dress-up and comfort parts: power windows, six-way adjustable seating, extra light groups, premium audio equipment, and extra-cost trim.

Following this are oddball or rarely seen parts; due to the sales bank nature of Superbirds, few actually had much additional equipment, so there is novelty to noting a component not present on many others. Singularly, these things may not add a significant value beyond the attraction of the engine, driveline, and basic interior options, but as a package, the more options a car has, the better.

"Desirable" Paint Colors

The exterior paint option requires a little more insight. Paint is often a personal preference, but the cars finished in one of the HIP colors (EK2 Vitamin "C" Orange, FJ5 Lime Light Green, or FY1 Lemon Twist Yellow), EV2 Tor-Red, or special-order 999 Corporate Blue are likely attractive to more potential buyers, even though the scarce Petty-inspired 999 code is probably the only color that commands a premium. A car documented to have been done in FK5 (Deep Burnt Orange Metallic, the factory error color) is almost in its own class due to sheer rarity.

RESTORING A SUPERBIRD

Of course, for enthusiasts who have ended up owning a Superbird that is either not complete or needs refinishing, self-restoration can become the end goal due to simple finances. Before going further, if you consider the car as an investment, this job is not recommended for the inexperienced or even non-professional rebuilding shop. To attain its final worth in the modern marketplace, the car requires proper completion.

If the end result is a car that needs to be re-restored due to non-professional or incomplete personal efforts, this is a poor choice. On the other hand, if you simply want to be able to note that you did it yourself, it is your car, so you can do as you please. Just do not expect it to showcase value equal to that of an identical car done by a well-focused restoration shop, one that has both the experience and the paid artisans to do each job properly.

Disassembly Documentation

Regardless of who does it, as in any restoration effort, it is important to follow the protocols of documenting all disassembly. This should entail photographic evidence of any factory marks to be reapplied after painting, organizing components for refreshing, a list of replacement pieces required, and proper storage of

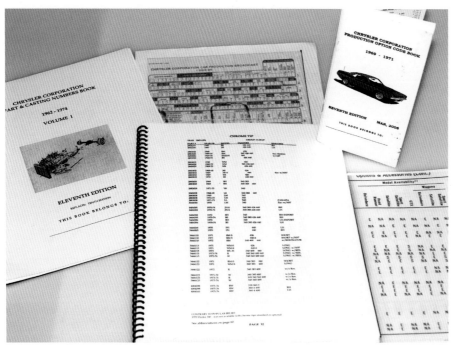

Today, sources to understand factory coding, options, and part numbers are available. These books from Galen's Tag Service allow anyone with a broadcast sheet to learn which parts are correct for the car owned or being documented.

everything to prevent loss or damage. It is critical to understand that high-demand missing parts even on a nearly complete car can take years and tens of thousands of dollars to obtain. For this reason among others, serious restorers usually want to start with a complete, fully-assembled car so they can document it to their liking, not one that is already a full-size Revell model kit, possibly with missing parts.

The body presents the normal challenges if rust is present in the cowl or rear window corners, as these are difficult repairs even for experienced body men. This is why cars sold from dry, arid states are noted as such; rust is not a major issue. Missing body stampings specific to A13 Superbird construction add major costs to the restoration. Some parts are not being reproduced and require refreshed donor items removed from another original A13 vehicle. Therefore, it is important

to work from as much reference material as possible, certainly beyond the scope of this introductory look at the model.

The full factory list of replacement parts and their numbers appears in the appendix. If possible, research the details on any missing or irreparable parts before completing a purchase. Many sellers are forthright as to why a car was left undone before selling it, but others may not be. Do not make the expensive mistake of overpaying for a project that is already stripped of the important components, especially the inner nose and wing supports, exterior components, or the rear window plug.

Fit and Finish

When the car is ready to be reassembled following bodywork, paint prep, and paint, the restorer will use techniques both in general terms and specific to the A13 cars that are part of this process. Due to changes in paint pigments, cars today are often panel-painted before reassembly. This is an area of increased scrutiny for the discriminating buyer, and fit and finish have never been more important, or as expensive. Good automotive painters receive premiums for their efforts.

Date-Coded Components

Turning to the driveline, most original date-coded components for Chrysler performance cars built in late 1969 (in the first three months of 1970-model production) are exceedingly rare today. Regardless of whether you are procuring your own parts or a shop is doing it, again we are talking values in the thousands of dollars for some parts. These can include

On the banking at Atlanta Motor Speedway, viewed from the passenger's side of the Ramo Stott #7 Superbird. Enjoyment is a big part of owning a collector car and driving on select occasions at places for which the car was bred is especially satisfying for Superbird owners.

capable of duplicating both show car level and OEM-level finishes, often with proprietary processes. Their costs are in line with that expertise. Among these are OEM-correct finishes found on brake drums, exhaust parts, wiring components, suspension pieces, etc., all which play into final value. Conversely, a shop noted for attention to general automotive detail might not be as exclusive or expensive, but may also change or reconstruct things without recognizing what is right.

A seriously executed restoration of any Chrysler aero model found incomplete or in poor condition usually takes years to redo. As a result, some people find that working on a car that was previously restored, if done properly at that time, may be less expensive to upgrade to modern standards compared to a more decrepit but original example that may require more effort to complete. That stated, it is still important to understand exactly which pieces in particular on the A13 package (driveline, hardware, and body) should already be on any car being considered for purchase to prevent expensive surprises.

correct Hemi carburetors and other specific parts that also fit similar-performance B- and E-Body vehicles factory-created in the same time frame.

Listing the exact casting number and time frames for these parts is beyond the scope of this book, but casting number reference books, factory parts lists, interchange manuals, and honest resellers of components are of great value. In addition to detailing, there will also be mechanical costs with any engine or transmission rebuilding to consider. Serious buyers check everything for originality.

The End Product Is What You Pay For . . .

Any car restoration usually ends up being a combination of your desires and what you are willing to pay for. The most experienced and expensive shops are

In conclusion, although it is not easy, the reward of Superbird ownership often outweighs these challenges. As a hobbyist, if you have a car that you intend to refinish or are considering buying, I recommend that you discuss your possibilities with people who have knowledge of the cars. There are groups devoted to aero models, experts in restoration and provenance, and individuals with passionate enthusiasm. Take their advice to heart, and know that this is a unique group of collectors and aficionados who welcome newcomers who share their interests.

SUPERBIRD BY THE NUMBERS

The following final pages include information to help identify a Superbird. For more details, I recommend contacting Chrysler-associated restoration or verification sources for complete lists by component number or casting date.

Decoding a VIN Tag

As noted in chapter 2, the vehicle identification number was assigned to the car at the time it was scheduled to be built. This number is most easily found on top of the dash structure, visible through the driver's side of the windshield.

Ironically, the most important character on this tag is often the fifth alphanumeric stamping as read from the left. It is the character that denotes the engine design.

The final six characters are the sequentially assigned VIN number. In the case of the Superbird, those digits fall in the range between 149597 and 181274.

The final eight digits of the VIN were stamped in two locations on the body during its initial subassembly before painting: on the driver-side trunk lip under the weather stripping and usually (but not always) on the core support for the radiator.

The VIN is also found on the passenger-side pad of the engine and passenger-side front edge of the transmission.

All Superbirds have a VIN like this example: RM23(x)0A(xxxxxx). It decodes like this:

R	Midsize (B-Body platform) Plymouth brand
M	Medium-level (all Road Runners)
2	Two-door
3	Hardtop
(x)	U for 440 4-barrel, V for 440 6-barrel, or R for 426H 8-barrel
0	Model year 1970
A	Lynch Road plant
(xxxxx)	Assembly plant sequential numbers in a range between 149597 and 181274.

The six-digit assembly plant sequence was assigned numerically to every Chrysler product in every plant during the construction period, hence the large range among just 1,935 cars.

The sequence started each model year with 100001. Therefore, the first Superbird (149789) was the 49,789th vehicle that Chrysler assigned an assembly number to during the calendar year 1969. Generally speaking, all production Superbirds were built between October 17 and December 18. The final VIN, 181274, was the highest VIN input into the system for production, but it was not the last car built.

Decoding a Fender Tag

The fender tag is the most important physical identification tool on the car. Superbirds are unique in that they are sometimes found with the tag unpainted, meaning that the tag was not attached via a screw in the Metal Shop prior to painting. This tag was the primary guide to assembly-line workers to verify which options were to be installed; a tag and broadcast sheet should match. However, errors do creep in. It has been hypothesized that wrongly input initial data is the reason that a handful of Superbirds were painted FK5 (Burnt Orange Metallic) instead of the authorized FJ5 (Lime Light Green).

The tag is read from bottom to top. Therefore, the bottom line is first and denotes the driveline to be assembled by the Chassis and the Metal Shop. The line

The fender tag from the unrestored Superbird now in the Wellborn Musclecar museum. This was the initial guide for the assembly of the car.

This fender tag is on the rare FK5 Superbird on display at the Garlits Museum. Like the Wellborn car, the only major option this car received new was the C16 console. Otherwise, it was a standard 440 U-code A36 driveline and appears to have been a sales bank build-up, lending credence to the possibility that the handful of cars painted this color was due to a keystroke error during data input on Chrysler's mainframe computer. (Steve Reyes Photo)

also yields engine, transmission, engine/year/plant, and serial number information.

The following data is courtesy Galen Govier, *Chrysler Corporation Production Code Option Code Book 1969–1971*. He notes that Lynch Road fender tags are often devoid of specific options that are found on a broadcast sheet. Due to the tight time window for ordering and Lynch Road's austerity in tag information, there is one fender tag; I have not seen a Superbird with two fender tags.

LINE 1 (BOTTOM):
EXX DXX RM23 X0A 1XXXXX

Powerplant
Three engines were offered.

E86 Standard	440-ci 4-barrel Super Commando V-8 wedge engine
E87 +$249.55	440-ci 6-barrel 440 Six Pack V-8 wedge engine
E74 +$841.05	426-ci Hemi 8-barrel V-8 hemispherical engine

Transmission
Two transmissions were offered.

D32 Standard	A727 TorqueFlite 3-speed automatic
D21 w/ A33	A833 New Process 4-speed

Body Style
All are identical for Superbird.

RM23	R, B-Body; M, medium; 2, two-door; 3, hardtop

Engine, Year, Plant
All start with either U, V, or R. *Always* followed by 0 for 1970 and A for Lynch Road. For example: U0A, V0A, R0A.

Assembly Plant Sequential Number
Final six digits of the VIN. For example: 150000.

Sample line 1: E86 D32 RM23 U0A 163401 decodes to 440-4, Automatic, Two-Door Hardtop, U-Engine, 1970, Lynch Road, VIN Serial Number

LINE 2: AA1 A1A1 BB1 B30 J97111

The second line from the bottom of the fender tag begins with the external paint code, trim code, upper door paint code, scheduled production date, and internal vehicle ordering number.

AA1 Exterior Paint Code

Superbirds were limited to seven specific colors.

EB5	Blue Fire Metallic
EK2	Vitamin "C" Orange (HIP)
EW1	Alpine White
EV2	Tor-Red
FJ5	Lime Light Green (HIP)
FY1	Lemon Twist Yellow (HIP)
999	Corporate (Petty) Blue
FK5	Deep Burnt Orange Metallic (factory error)

A1A1 Interior Trim Level and Code

Two interior colors, black or white; codes are for either bench or bucket designs.

H2X9	Black vinyl bench seating
P6XA	Black vinyl bucket seating
H2XW	White vinyl bench seating
P6XW	White vinyl bucket seating

BB1 Interior Body Paint Code

Superbirds were limited to two options matching the interior color.

TX9	Black upper-body interior paint
EW1	White upper-body interior paint

Scheduled Vehicle Order Date

All Superbirds were given an official order date of November 30, 1969: Numerals 1 through 9 denoted months from January through September. Chrysler chose letters (A, B, C) for the final three months of the production year. (This fixed date on all cars may have been required to ensure NASCAR eligibility). The J-sequence order number following this superseded this date, allowing factory production control to determine an actual creation date for sequencing each car onto the Lynch Road assembly line.

B30	November 30, 1969

Vehicle Order Number

This is an internal tracking number. It appears on the October 7, 1969, NASCAR memo, and was initially assigned to properly track construction of the total number of a specific special-order model (in this case A13 Superbirds) into the production schedule. Because these 1,935 cars were limited to just three months early in the 1970 model production cycle, the company apparently chose to use 2,500 of the final 3,000 numbers on a 100,000-unit yearlong run. Therefore, Superbird numbers run from J97000 to somewhere above J99000; this has no reference value beyond comparison to similar numbers.

J97000 to J99499	Superbirds fall between these two control numbers

Sample line 2: FY1 P6XA TX9 B30 J97175 decodes to Lemon Twist HIP paint, Black Bucket Seats, Black Interior Upper-Door Paint, November 30 Scheduled Build Date, Vehicle Order Number J97175.

LINES 3 AND 4:
SALES AND OPTION CODES

The third and fourth lines from the bottom list the optional and standard equipment specific to the car; these are coded based on what could be added to a Superbird. Some items could not be ordered and are not found on the fender tag. They are as follows:

A01	Light package
A04	Basic group (included in A13)
A31/ A32/A34	Performance axle packages (lower-gear ratios)
A35	Trailer towing package
D91	Sure-Grip (included in A33/A36 axle package)
F25	70-amp battery (included as standard and not to be ordered again)
H31	Rear defroster (due to rear plug installation)
H51	Air conditioning
L42	Headlamp delay
M25	Sill molding
N96	Air Grabber
R31	Rear speaker (due to rear plug installation)
V21	Hood paint

Some items were standard and are coded on all Superbird fender tags.

V19	Special-order black vinyl top (coded as standard V1X on some early cars)
V-88	Transverse stripe delete (Road Runner standard dust trail for 1970)
26	26-inch radiator (all Superbirds used this unit as part of the max cooling system)

Sample lines 3 and 4: V19-V-88 26 C16 decodes as the three standard codes and one extra option, the C16 console.

LINE 5: 111 011 611: DRIVELINE CODES

The fifth line from the bottom gave specifics on Superbird driveline specifications beyond the information noted on line 1 above. Research by the Daytona-Superbird Auto Club brought this to light; it consists of three three-character strings.

111 Engine Code

Superbirds could be ordered with three possible engines, in either automatic or manual transmission configuration.

112	426 8-barrel, 4-speed
113	426 8-barrel, automatic
114	440 4-barrel, 4-speed
115	440 4-barrel, automatic (standard)
122	440 6-barrel, 4-speed
123	440 6-barrel, automatic

011 Differential Code

Two axle designs were part of the A33 and A36 Performance Axle Packages.

052	Chrysler 8¾-inch design, 3.55:1 ratio, Sure-Grip (standard)
083	Dana 60 9¾-inch design, 3.54:1 ratio, Sure-Grip

611 Transmission Code

Two designs were possible with the A33 and A36 Performance Axle Packages, but some examples received the internally stronger A727 automatic transmission (671/672). The A833 4-speed was identical regardless of engine design.

670	440 4-barrel, automatic (standard A727)
671	426 8-barrel, Hemi Automatic
672	440 6-barrel, automatic (as above Hemi)
676	426 8-barrel, 440 6-speed, 440 4-speed

Sample line 5: 115 052 670 decodes to 440 4-Barrel Automatic Carb, 8¾ Differential, 440 4-barrel A727 Automatic.

LINE 6 (TOP): 11111 222222: GATE AND ASSEMBLY CODES

The line farthest from the bottom on the tag shows two numeric strings, one five-digit and one six-digit. Each is exclusive to a single car. Used at Lynch Road, the five-digit code is the Gate Number, referring to the specific sidegates used for initial body assembly. Greg Lane of maxwedge.com notes that in this time period, as many as 32 such gates were in use at Lynch Road. The gate is not a doorway but an assembly-line rigging tool created to ensure proper panel alignment when the inner fenders, roof, and other components were added and welded to the base unibody frame for each body style.

It is possible that the Superbird was assigned more than one gate; it is also probable but unknown if the standard RM23 Belvedere hardtop gates used for Road Runner builds were compatible with these cars or if special gates were designed for them. The first two numbers denote the gate; the final three numbers are the daily sequencing number through that gate, which began at 101 each day. Therefore, a car showing the code 20143 was built using gate 20 and was the 43rd car built on that gate on that day.

The second numeric string is the Line Sequence Number used on Lynch Road cars but actually denoting the yearlong sequencing of bodies into Chrysler's computer system. Again, likely used on the fender tags at this particular plant to facilitate assembly efficiencies, this number is not identical to the VIN but is somewhere close to it due to the short production window on these cars. Because of the sheer volume of cars that were built in this facility, the tag reference is probably an additional way that the assembly line at Lynch Road could be managed. For all Superbirds, this number is identical to the first sequence number found on the upper left corner of the broadcast sheet.

Sample line 6: 15147 163140 decodes to Gate 15, 47th Construction On That Day, and 1969 Yearlong Construction Sequence.

Decoding a Broadcast Sheet

As discussed in chapter 2, each car received multiple broadcast sheets as it went through the assembly process. They were marked identically in terms of equipment. Most of them were discarded as work was completed on the line, although examples were sometimes left inside certain subassemblies such as seat backs or glovebox tops, or under the carpet or headliner. However, this was not deliberate. In fact, the government later mandated that production-line broadcast sheets could not be left anywhere inside a vehicle because of potential fire hazard. It's fortunate that these important "maps" to a car's construction happen to coincide with the creation of muscle cars such as the Superbird. Galen Govier's *Chrysler Corporation Production Code Option Code Book 1969–1971* is an important resource for checking these numbers, as was the Plymouth salesman booklet for 1970 showing all Road Runner options.

The sheet is standardized in two parts: six upper lines that show information used on the Metal Engine and Trim lines, and six lower lines that highlight specifics mainly used on the Final Line. You read the sheet from left to right and from top to bottom.

LINE 1:
VEHICLE CONSTRUCTION INFORMATION

Sequence Number
Lynch Road internal code begins with B (November) followed by the six-digit number Line Sequence Number found on the top line of the fender tag.

Vehicle Order Number
The assigned date (B30) and J-number sequence J97000–J99499 match line 5 of the fender tag.

Vehicle Identification Number
The VIN as found on the dash and elsewhere.

Vehicle Delivery Handling

Y05	Build to U.S. Specs
Y07	Build to Canada Specs
Y09	Build to Specs for Export
Y11	Domestic Publications
Y13	Dealer Demo
Y14	Sold Car
Y15	Direct Sale

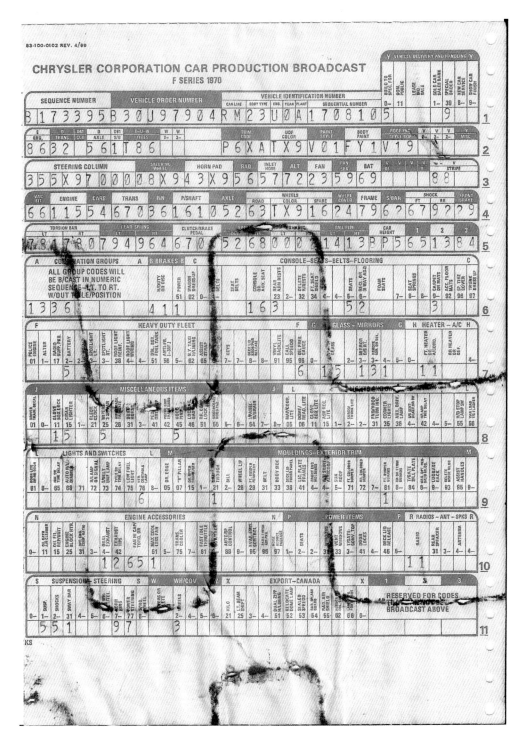

A sample broadcast sheet, courtesy of Frank Badalson. More complex than the window sticker or the fender tag, this gave specific build instructions to each section of the car's assembly and subassembly. Multiple copies were printed, one for each area of plant production.

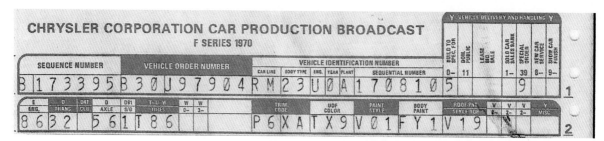

Lines 1 and 2 of the broadcast addressed vehicle identification, sequencing and special data, as well as basic engine, driveline, wheel, and paint for rapid comparison on the line.

Y16	Sales Bank
Y17	Corporate Lease Car System
Y22	Corporate Lease Car, Executive
Y28	Company Car/Public Relations
Y33	Fleet Sales
Y39	Special Order, All Superbirds
Y54	Chrysler Management Employee Purchase
Y91	Show Car Finish A/Less Gas
Y92	Show Car Finish B/Less Gas
Y97	Show Car Finish, 3 Gallons Gas Y05

LINE 2: CONSTRUCTION CONTINUED

E/Eng: Engine Code

74	426 Hemi 2x4-barrel V-8 425 hp (value - E74)
86	440-ci 4-barrel V-8 (High Performance) 375 hp (value - E86)
87	440-ci 3x2-barrel V-8 (High Performance) 390 hp (value - E87)

D/Trans: Transmission Code

21	4-speed manual (value - D21)
32	Heavy-duty automatic (value - D32; also see line 4)

D41: Clutch (with D21)
Blank (all MT Superbirds came with heavy-duty as standard).

D/Axle: Axle Package (value 56 - all Superbirds)

56	3.54:1/3.55:1 rear-axle ratio

D91 S/G: Sure-Grip (value 1 - all Superbirds)

1	Sure-Grip (value - D91)

T-U-W/Tires: Tire Design and Size (this dictated wheel dimension)

T86	F70-14 White sidewall
T87	F70-14 Raised white-letter Polyglas
U84	F60-15 Raised white-letter Polyglas GT

W0/W3: Spare Delete (Likely N/A Superbird)

W07	Delete spare tire (value - W07)

Trim Code: Interior Trim Code

H2 X9	Black vinyl bench seating
P6 XA	Black vinyl bucket seating
H2 XW	White vinyl bench seating
P6 XW	White vinyl bucket seating

UDF Color (upper door-frame paint code)

TX9	Black upper-body interior paint
EW1	White upper-body interior paint

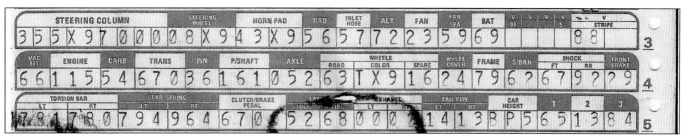

Lines 3, 4, and 5 were for the Chassis and Engine lines, denoting the exact components needed for the suspension and driveline, as well as steering trim.

Paint Style (V01- all Superbirds)

V01	Monotone

Body Paint: Exterior Paint Code

EB5	Blue Fire Metallic
EK2	Vitamin "C" Orange (HIP)
EW1	Alpine White
EV2	Tor-Red
FJ5	Lime Light Green (HIP)
FY1	Lemon Twist Yellow (HIP)
999	Corporate (Petty) Blue
FK5	Deep Burnt Orange Metallic (factory error)

Roof Paint, Top Style: Roof Style (V19 or V1X, all Superbirds)

V19	Special-order vinyl top /V1X some early cars

V2-V2-V2-Y

	Additional trim codes N/A on A13 Superbird

LINE 3: TRIM AND CHASSIS

Steering Column

315	B-Body manual shift
351	B-Body column-shift automatic

355	B-Body floor-shift automatic
X9	Black color
7000	Power steering column
7005	Power steering column with time-delay light
7085	Power steering column, time-delay light, automatic speed control

Steering Wheel

08	Standard partial-ring S79 wheel
10	Rim-Blow two-spoke S83 wheel (none known)
16	Woodgrain sport three-spoke S81 wheel
X9	Black
TT	Woodgrain with 16

Horn Pad

11	Rim switch pad (S83, none known)
43	Partial ring pad
47	Center cap pad
X9	Black, all Superbirds

Radiator (value 56 - all Superbirds)

56	26-inch radiator, PN2998956

Inlet Hose

57	Upper hose 26-inch radiator, 440 ci, PN2863257
86	Upper hose 26-inch radiator, 426 ci, PN2806186

Alternator

72	37-amp single pulley (non-air performance model), PN3438172
76	37-amp dual-pulley Hemi application model, PN3438176

Fan Design

16	Seven-blade Torque Drive (all manual, all Hemi), PN2863216
23	Seven-blade solid drive, PN2863223

For cooling reasons, Superbirds built after November 5 with E86/E87 and automatic drivelines used a solid-drive fan, not the seven-blade clutch-type unit.

Fan Spacer/clutch

59	1.06-inch aluminum spacer 383/440-ci, PN1851959 (see special note above with fan 23)
70	Torque-drive unit, PN2806070

Battery (value 69 - all Superbirds)

69	Mopar 70-amp red cap, PN2642969 (440/426 engine)

V08-V-V-V5

	Additional Trim, N/A Superbird

V Stripe (value 88 - all Superbirds)

88	Transverse stripe delete (value - V-88)

LINE 4: ENGINE AND CHASSIS

Power Brake Vacuum Fitting (value - 66)

66	Big-block vacuum fitting

Engine

112	426 8-barrel, 4-speed
113	426 8-barrel, automatic
114	440 4-barrel, 4-speed
115	440 4-barrel, automatic
122	440 6-barrel, 4-speed
123	440 6-barrel, automatic

Carburetor

00	Carter AFB; 4742 front; 4745S rear; 426H, manual
00	Carter AFB; 4742 front; 4746S rear; 426H, automatic
47	Holley 2-barrel; R4375A center; 440-6, manual
48	Holley 2-barrel; R4376A center; 440-6, automatic
49	Holley 2-barrel; R4373A center; 440-6, manual ECS (Cailfornia)
53	Carter AVS; 4738S; 440, manual
54	Carter AVS; 4738S; 440, automatic
58	Carter AVS; 4740S; 440, automatic; ECS (Cailfornia)

Transmission

670	440 4-barrel, automatic
671	426H 8-barrel, heavy-duty automatic
672	440 6-barrel, heavy-duty automatic
676	426 8-barrel, 440 6-barrel; 440 4-speed

Speedometer Pinion (value 36 - all Superbirds)

36	3.5 final ratio, red, F70-14/F60-15 tire sizes, PN2538936

Propeller Shaft (driveshaft)

161	3.25x51.5, 8.75; both 440, automatic, PN2996161
560	3.25x50.39, 9.75; both 440, manual; all 426, PN2995560

Rear Axle Assembly

052	A13 package, 3.55 Sure-Grip, 8.75-inch
083	A13 package, 3.54 Sure-Grip, 9.75-inch Dana

Road Wheel Design

17	14x6 steel, PN3420978
28	15x7 steel wheel, PN2944450
61	14x5.5 Rallye
63	14x5.5 five-spoke road wheel (Magnum 500)
71	15x7 Rallye

Wheel Color

TX9	Black (also used for spare w/ optional wheels)
EB5	Blue Fire Metallic
EK2	Vitamin "C" Orange (HIP)
EW1	Alpine White
EV2	Tor-Red
FJ5	Lime Light Green (HIP)
FY1	Lemon Twist Yellow (HIP)
999	Corporate (Petty) Blue

Spare Wheel

16	14x6, PN3420978
28	15x7, PN2944450

Wheel Cover (hubcap)

00	14-inch wire wheel cover, PN2944400
22	15-inch brushed Rallye wheel trim ring, PN3461222
24	14-inch brushed wheel trim ring (road and Rallye), PN2944424
43	15-inch chrome Rallye wheel trim ring, PN3461043
88	Dog dish, small cover, PN2944088

Frame

79	1970 B-Body w/ skid plate, PN3466479
94	1970 Hemi body w/ skid plate, PN2962094

S/Bar (value 62 - all Superbirds)

62	.88-inch diameter, all B-Body 1970–1972, PN2835862

Front Shock (value 67 - all Superbirds)

67	Heavy-duty model, PN3004969 (cast number, 2462067)

Rear Shock (value 92 - all Superbirds)

92	Heavy-duty model, PN2585618 (cast number, 2834892) or PN2834895 (cast number, 3400592)

Front Brakes (value 29 - all Superbirds)

29	Front disc brakes

LINE 5: CHASSIS

Torsion Bar (driver's side)

781	41x.92–inch diameter, brown paint (all 440/426 B-Body models), PN1857781

Torsion Bar (passenger's side)

780	41x.92–inch diameter, brown paint (all 440/426 B-Body models), PN1857780

Rear Springs (driver's side)

794	6-leaf spring, PN3004767

Rear Springs (passenger's side)

964	5-leaf spring, PN2004768

Clutch Pedal

63	4-speed, power brakes
67	Automatic, power brakes
68	Automatic, power brakes w/ speed control

Brake Pedal

00	No clutch, standard brake pedal
01	No clutch, J41 brake pedal dress-up
20	4-speed, standard pedal
21	4-speed, J41 clutch pedal dress-up

Labels, Idle: Decal with Idle Emissions

15	440 6-barrel, PN3577715
16	426 Hemi, 4-speed, PN3577716
17	426 Hemi, auto, PN3577717
18	440 6-barrel, PN3412418
30	426 Hemi, automatic, PN3512030
31	426 Hemi, 4-speed, PN3512031
52	440 4-barrel, automatic, PN3462552
53	440 4-barrel, 4-speed, PN3462553

Labels/Tire: Decals with tire pressure

68	F60x15, PN3402068 (this may have been a default code on performance B-Bodies)

Driver-Side Exhaust

Main before muffler, left (value 00 - all Superbirds).

00	All Superbirds used H-pipe, N/A

Passenger-Side Exhaust

Main before muffler, right.

02	B/RB dual-exhaust H-pipe, PN3404802
70	Hemi pipe w/ intake connection, H-pipe, PN2781270

Driver-Side Tailpipe

Muffler to tip end left; all Hemi cars received N42 resonaters.

03	440 left-hand w/o N42 tip, PN3404003
	440 left-hand w/ N42 tip, PN3404014
	426H left-hand w/ N42, PN3404011

Passenger-Side Tailpipe

Muffler to tip end, right.

09	426H right-hand w/ N42, PN3404012
10	440 right-hand w/o N42 tip, PN3404810
	440 right-hand w/ N42 tip, PN3404013

Car Height

Suspension/vehicle build height is based on ground clearance (value BP5 - all Superbirds).

BP5	Standard B-Body layout

1-2-3

Box 1, Master Brake Info: Info on braking system master cylinder.

65	Power disc brakes
66	Power disc brakes, Hemi car

Box 2, Sheet Print Hour (01-23 military standard time format): Hour for specific sheet.

04, 4:00am; 10, 10:00am; 14, 2:00pm; 20, 8:00pm; etc.

Box 3, Sheet Print Sequence (00–99): Placement of Specific Sheet Print Output.

04, 4th in sequence; 36, 36th in sequence; etc.

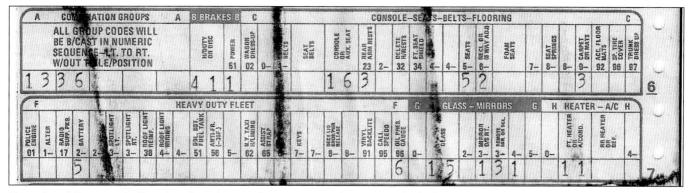

Lines 6 and 7 covered all optional equipment between A and H, many of which were interior-related.

LINE 6

A. Combination Groups (A13 - all Superbirds)

A13	Special NASCAR RM23 Plymouth Belvedere Road Runner. All Superbirds also have one of the following
	A33: Track Pak Axle Option w/ 9.75 Dana 60 differential, 3.54 Sure-Grip, Maximum Cooling package, 7-blade torque-drive fan, Hemi-grade suspension, manual transmission car; A33 excludes any A/C option.
	A36: Performance Axle Package Option w/ 8.75 banjo-design differential, 3.55 Sure-Grip, Maximum Cooling package, 7-blade torque-drive fan (changed to solid drive on A13 built after November 5, 1969), Hemi-grade suspension, automatic transmission; A13/A36 combination excludes any A/C option.

B. Brakes (value 41, 1 - all Superbirds)

41	Front Disc brakes w/ heavy-duty rear drums (value - B41)
1	Power-assist brakes (value - B51)

C. Console, Seats, Belts, Flooring

02	Wagon dress-up, N/A
0	N/A
1	Shoulder Belts

3	Front shoulder belts; driver and passenger (value - C13)
4	Rear shoulder belts; driver and passenger (value - C14)

Seat Belts

5	Deluxe belt option buckle dress-up, warning lamps, brackets (value - C15)

Console or Auxiliary Seat

6	Center console (value - C16)	
1	Center cushion/armrest (buddy seat) (value - C21)	
23	Rear Armrest	
	3	Armrest w/ ashtray (value - C23)
2	N/A	
32	Delete Head Rests, N/A	
34	Front Seat Shield, N/A	
4	N/A	
5	Seats (front)	
	1	Bench seat split 50/50 (value - C51)
	5	Bucket seats (value - C55)
6	Seats	
	2	Driver bucket six-way adjustable (value - C62)
	5	Bench seat extra-cushion air foam (value - C65)

7	N/A	
8	Seat Springs	
9	Carpet or Mats	
	3	Carpeting (all Superbirds carpeted) (value - C93)
92	Accessory Floor Mats	
	2	Heavy-duty front and rear, black (value - C92)
96	N/A	
97	N/A	

LINE 7

F. Heavy-Duty Fleet

01	Police Engine, N/A	
1	Alternator (N/A, all Superbirds standard with heavy-duty models)	
17	Radio Suppression Package	
	7	Radio suppression package (value - F17)
2	Battery (value, 25; all Superbirds)	
	5	Mopar heavy-duty 70-amp series 27, black w/ red caps (value - F25)
2	N/A	
3	Spotlight: driver's side, N/A	
3	Spotlight: passenger's side, N/A	
38	Roof Light Reinforcement (police option) N/A	
4	Roof Light Wiring, N/A	
4	N/A	
51	Double-Bottom Fuel Tank	
56	Anti-Freeze (-35F), extreme-cold antifreeze treatment (value - F56, used on all Y07 cars to Canada)	
5	N/A	
62	New York Taxi H/Lining, N/A	
65	Assist Strap	
6	N/A	
7	Keys	
2	Single Key Package for door/trunk/ign (value - F72); no known examples	
7	NA	

7	N/A	
8	Decklid Knob, power release	
8	N/A	
91	Vinyl Backlite (convertibles, N/A)	
95	California Speedometer	
96	Oil Pressure Gauge (value, 6; all Superbirds)	
	6	Oil pressure gauge in dash (value - F96)

G. Glass, Mirrors

0	N/A Superbird	
Glass	11	Solex tinted, all windows; clear backlight on all Superbirds (value - G11)
	15	Solex tinted windshield only (value - G15)
2	N/A	
3	Mirror Outside Passenger	
	1	Manual passenger-side outside mirror, chrome (value - G31)
3	Remote Mirror or Delete	
	3	Standard driver-side outside mirror, chrome (value - G33)
	6	Remote driver-side mirror w/ passenger-side standard mirror (value - G36)
4	Rearview Mirror	
	1	Prismatic rearview mirror (value - G41)
	2	Standard rearview mirror (standard G42; not coded)
5	N/A	

H. Heater, A/C

0	N/A
	Front Heater or A/C
11	Heater, front (value - H11)
	Rear Heater or Defrost; rear unit N/A on Superbird
4	N/A

LINE 8

J. Miscellaneous Items

01	Drivertrain Decal	
0	N/A	
11	Glove Box Lock	
	1	Locking glove box door (value - J11)

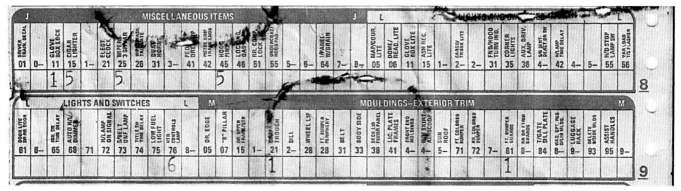

Lines 8 and 9 covered options under the J-L-M areas, which were mainly lights and dress-up pieces.

15	Cigar Lighter	
	5	Cigar lighter in dash (value - J15)
1	N/A	
21	Electric Clock	
	1	Clock in dash, N/A w/ N95 tach/clock (value - J21)
25	Wiper 3-Speed/Variable	
	5	3-speed windshield wiper (value - J25)
28	Wiper/Wash Tailgate, N/A	
31	Dual Horns, N/A Road Runner	
3	N/A	
41	Pedal Dress-Up	
	1	Pedal dress-up trim (value - J41)
42	Pistol Grip Transmission Knob	
	2	Blank; Hurst Pistol Grip (value - J42 but is left blank, as all were 4-speeds)
45	Hood Pins (value - 45 - all Superbirds)	
	5	Hood pins (value - J45)
46	Locking Gas Cap	
	6	Locking gas cap (value - J46)
51	Rear Compartment Lock, N/A	
55	Undercoat/Hood Pad	
5	Undercoating/Hood Insulation (value - J55), N/A	
6	N/A	
64	Instrument Panel w/ woodgrain interior trim, N/A	
7	N/A	
8	N/A (all spoilers part of A13 not marked on the sheet)	

L. Lighting and Switches

05	Map/Courtesy Light (underdash mounted), A01 (N/A Superbird)
06	Dome/Read Light (underroof mounted)
11	Glove Box Light, in-box mounted A01 only
15	Ash Rec. Light, in-dash mounted A01 only
1	N/A
2	Cargo Trunk Light, A01 only
2	N/A
31	Fender Hood Turn Indicator, N/A Superbird
35	Corner Lights, N/A
36	Aux Driving Lamp, N/A
4	S/G Sent. Deact. Dr Sw
42	H/Lamp Time Delay, N/A Superbird
4	N/A
5	N/A
55	H/D Stop Lamp Sw
56	Variable Load T/S Flasher

LINE 9

L. Lights and Switches (continued)

61	Door Lite SW RR Door, rear door light, N/A Superbird

6	N/A	
65	Ignition Switch Time Delay	
68	N/A	
71	N/A	
72	H/Lamp on Signal	
73	S/Belt Unf Lamp	
	3	Seat belt light, included with C15 pedal order (value - L73)
74	N/A	
75	Low-Fuel Light	
76	Heater Controls Lamp	
	6, standard all 1970 B-Body (value - L76)	
8	N/A	

M. Moldings and Exterior Trim

05	Door-Edge Molding	
	5	Chrome door-edge moldings (value - N05)
07	B-Pillar Molding, N/A Superbird hardtop	
15	Door Upper Frame/Qtr: four-door molding, N/A Superbird	
1	N/A	
21	Drip Trough, N/A Superbird	
2	Sill, N/A Superbird (value - M25)	
26	Wheel Lip, N/A Superbird	
28	Front Bumper Periphery, N/A Superbird	
31	Belt	
	1	Belt-line molding (value - M31)
33	Body Side, N/A Superbird	
38	Deck Lid Finish Panel, N/A Superbird	
41	License Plate Frames, N/A Superbird	
4	Front-End Moldings, N/A Superbird	
	4	w/ Skirt Airscoop, N/A
5	Sun Roof, N/A Superbird	
71	Front Colored Bumper, N/A Superbird	
72	Rear Colored Bumper, N/A Superbird	
7	N/A Superbird	
81	Front Bumper Guards (value 1- all Superbirds)	
	1	Front bumper guards (denoted the rubber/steel nose strip) (value - M81)

8	Rear or Front/Rear Bumper Guards	
	3	Rear bumper guards (value - M83)
	5	Both (but not used on Superbird due to M81 inclusiveness) (value - M85)
84	N/A Superbird	
8	N/A Superbird	
9	Luggage Rack, N/A Superbird	
93	Delete w/ Side Molding; Related M33, N/A Superbird	
95	Assist Handles; none known to exist	
	9	N/A Superbird

LINE 10

N. Engine Accessories

0	N/A	
11	N/A	
15	Oil Fil. Rep/Unit	
25	Eng Block Heater	
31	Optional Engine Compression Ratio, N/A	
3	N/A	
4	Dual Exhaust (value 1 - all Superbirds)	
	1	Dual exhaust (value - N41)
42	Exhaust Tips	
	2	Chrome exhaust tips (value - N42)
	Fan High-Capacity/Torque-drive (value 65 - all Superbirds)	
	65	Torque-drive fan (value - N65 including those with non-TD fan/spacer)
51	Max Cool, less fan (value 1 - all Superbirds)	
	1	Maximum cooling (value - N51)
	5	N/A
75	Trans Cooler (N75 was on Hemi automatics but not coded)	
7	N/A	
81	Fast Idle Throttle	
8	Governor/Tachometer	
	5	Tachometer Tic Toc Tach (value - N85)
88	Automatic Speed Control	
	8	440 4-barrel only (value - N88)
9	N/A Superbird	
95	Evaporative Emissions Control	
	5	California Delivery (value - N95)
96	Carb Fresh Air Package, N/A Superbird	
97	Noise Reduction Package, N/A Superbird	

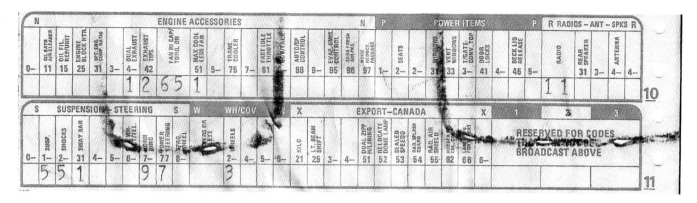

Lines 10 and 11 covered engine accessories, power and audio components, and final suspension parts. Special final notes and export instructions are here as well.

P. Power Items

1	N/A	
2	Seats	
2	Power Seats, N/A Superbird	
31	Windows	
	1	Power windows (value - P31)
33	Vent Windows, N/A Superbird	
3	Tailgate Convertible Top, N/A Superbird	
41	Door Locks	
4	N/A	
45	Deck Lid Release	
5	N/A	

R. Radio, Antennas, Speakers

11	AM Radio (value - R11)
13	AM Radio, heavy-duty 5.5-watt (value - R13)
21	AM/FM Stereo (value - R21)
22	AM Stereo eight-Track Player (value - R22)
31	Rear Speaker (N/A Superbird, but one is known to exist)
3	N/A
4	Antennae, standard w/ radio
4	N/A

LINE 11

S. Suspension and Steering

| 0 | N/A |

S. Suspension and Steering

1	Suspension (value 15 - all Superbirds)	
	15	Extra-heavy-duty/Hemi (value - S15)
2	Shocks (value 25 - all Superbirds)	
	25	1-inch heavy-duty front/rear (value - S25)
31	Sway Bar (value 1 - all Superbirds)	
	31	Front sway bar (value - S31)
34	Front Seat Shield, N/A Superbird	
4	N/A	
5	N/A	
6	Steering Wheel Tilt/Telescopic, N/A Superbird	
7	Horn Ring	
	9	Horn ring, partial (value - S79)
77	Power Steering (value 7 - all Superbirds)	
	7	Power steering (value - S77)
8	Steering Wheel	
	1	Woodgrain sports three-spoke (value - S81)
	3	Rim-Blow two-spoke (value S83 - none known)
	4	Blank, standard design, three-spoke (value - S84)

W. Wheels and Wheel Covers

Covers or Delete

| 11 | 14-inch deluxe (full) wheel covers (value - W11) |
| 15 | 14-inch wire wheel covers (value - W15) |

Wheels

2	Standard 14- or 15-inch steel (not coded)
1	Rallye Wheel 14- or 15-inch Rallye w/ trim ring (value - W21)
3	Road Wheel 14-inch Magnum 500 design (value - W23)

X. Export to Canada

21	Kilo	
	1	240-km speedometer (value - X21)
25	Beam Shift	
	5	Driver-side headlamp beam shift, export (value - X25)
3	N/A Superbird	
4	N/A Superbird	
51	Zipper Headliner, N/A Superbird	
52	Related to X51, N/A Superbird	
53	Sealed Speedometer	
54	Radiator Splash Guard, N/A Superbird	
55	Radiator Air Shield, N/A Superbird	
62	Rubber Str Col Coupler, N/A Superbird	
66	Label Manufactured for Export	
8	N/A Superbird	

1 – 2 – 3

Reserved for codes that cannot be broadcast above.

Window Sticker

The Monroney label, or window sticker, was sometimes saved with the owner's paperwork. It listed the car's optional equipment and included pricing. Some components were standard and had no numeric value added (as shown in the example).

The top two lines showed the plant, VIN, and special-order information. At left was a color code and trim code for quick identification. Next came the origi-

nating dealer and shipping location, usually identical.

It also showed the basic package and price ($4,298 here), optional equipment and associated costs (in this case, almost $500), a subtotal and destination charge ($22 on this example that only had to go as far as Ohio).

This example, at $4,782 with Road Runner–level creature comforts, was an expensive investment for a late-1969 or early-1970 buyer, not to mention the insurance premiums that the big-block option automatically entailed at the time.

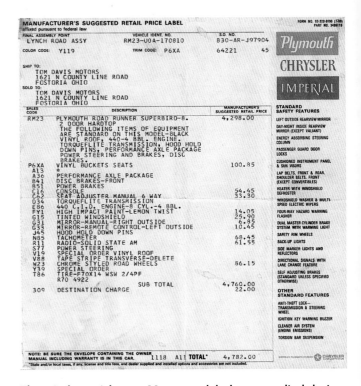

The window sticker, or Monroney label, was applied during final assembly at Lynch Road. If missing or stolen from a car when new, the dealership had to go back to Chrysler for a reprint.

The document (81-690-0895) reproduced here (with permission from FCA LLC) dated March 1970 shows exploded Superbird parts views and number lists for the dealership parts department. This rare original is courtesy of the Frank Badalson Collection.

SUPER BIRD
PARTS LIST

MARCH
1970

PARTS DIVISION ★ **CHRYSLER** MOTORS CORPORATION

Printed in U. S. A.

81-690-0895

This is the complete list of replacement components and associated part numbers as released by Chrysler in March 1970. This is invaluable for identifying by number each part needed for these special cars. (Dodge, Plymouth, and the AMC design are registered trademarks of FCA US LLC.)

SUPER BIRD

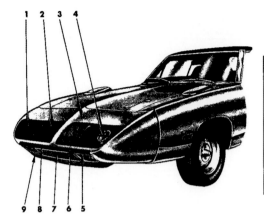

1970 SUPER BIRD

REF. NO.	PART NUMBER	DESCRIPTION
1-	3571 170-1	DECAL
2-	3571 178-9	DECAL
3-	3571 101	NOSE CONE Complete
3-	3571 192	NOSE CONE (Sheet Metal only)
4-	3505 138-9	DECAL
5-	3571 146-7	FRAME
6-	3571 174	RUB STRIP
7-	3571 156	PANEL
8-	3571 157	FRAME
9-	3412 616	SPOILER

19a3316

REF. NO.	PART NUMBER	DESCRIPTION
10-	3571110	VINYL ROOF BLACK
11-	3571106-7	MOULDING
12-	3571138-9	VERTICAL STABILIZER
13-	3571137	HORIZONTAL STABILIZER
14-	3571108-9	MOULDING

REF. NO.	PART NUMBER	DESCRIPTION
15-	3571 142	DECAL BLACK
15-	3571 143	DECAL WHITE
16-	3571 114	DECAL BLACK
16-	3571 128	DECAL WHITE

SUPER BIRD
NOSE CONE

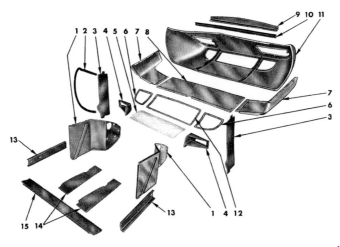

19a3317

FENDER-VALANCE-SCOOP

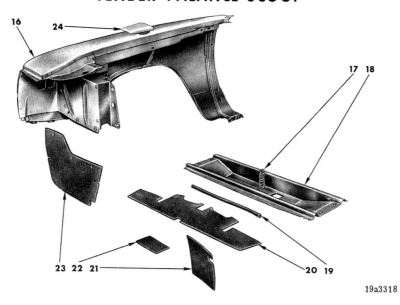

19a3318

SUPER BIRD
HEAD LAMP

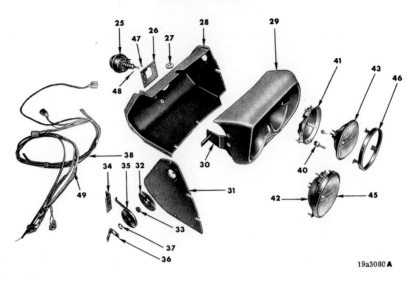

19a3080 **A**

REF. NO.	PART NO.	DESCRIPTION
1	3412 606-7	BULKHEAD
2	3571 162	SEAL
3	3571 163	SEAL
4	3571 154-5	BRACKET
5	3571 156	PANEL
6	3571 146-7	FRAME
7	3571 167-8	PANEL
8	3571 148	PANEL
9	3412 616	SPOILER
10	3571 174	TRIP
11	3571 192	NOSE CONE ASSY (SHEET METAL ONLY)
11	3571 101	NOSE CONE ASSY COMPLETE
12	3571 157	FRAME
13	3571 150-1	SUPPORT
14	3571 172	SEAL
15	3571 152	CROSSMEMBER
16	3571 158-9	FENDER
17	2935 375	SPRING
18	2949 874	CROSSBAR
19	3571 187	SEAL
20	3412 686	SEAL
21	3412 692	SEAL
22	3412 691	SEAL
23	3571 164	SEAL
24	3571 132-3	AIR SCOOP
25	2926 961	ACTUATOR

REF. NO.	PART NO.	DESCRIPTION
26	3412 636	PLATE
27	144 229	GROMMET
28	3412 682-3	COMPARTMENT
29	3412 620-1	HEADLAMP HSG.
30	3412 618	BRACKET
31	3412 666-7	PLATE
32	3412 631	CAP
33	6027 280	BUSHING
34	3412 694	BRACKET
35	3412 630	SPRING
36	6027 292	CLIP
37	1922 183	"C" CLIP
38	3571 160	WIRING
40	2785 842	ADJ. SCREW & NUT
41	2786 884-5	HIGH H/LAMP SEAT
42	2786 882-3	LOW H/LAMP SEAT
43	152 286	SEAL BEAM LOW
45	152 285	SEAL BEAM HIGH
46	2449 525	"J" RING
47	2857 976	SHAFT, CLIP
48	9416 049	SCREW
49	3412 675	VAC. HOSE 22" BLACK
49	3412 676	VAC. HOSE 22" YELLOW
49	3412 677	VAC. HOSE 16" BLACK
49	3412 678	VAC. HOSE 16" YELLOW
49A	2926 337	TUBE AND CONNECTOR H/LAMP DOOR VAC. CONTROL

ADDITIONAL PARTS LIST
(Not Illustrated)

QTY.	PART NO.	DESCRIPTION
1	3412 150-1	MLDG. W/S O/Side Finsh
1	3412 644	CAR JACK Front Wheel
1	3412 645	HANDLE Car Jack Front Wheel
1	3412 652	BRACKET Front License Plate Mtg.
AR	3412 684	BOLT Nose Cone
2	3412 687	CAP SCREW Stabilizer Attaching
AR	3412 693	POP Rivet
2	3412 698	SEAL Yoke To Radiator
1	3412 764-5	HEAD LAMP Door
1	3412 784-5	VERTICAL FIN Support Front
1	3412 790-1	VERTICAL FIN Support Rear
1	3571 103	HEADLINING Black
1	3571 104	SHELF Trim Panel Black
1	3571 105	MOULDING Rear Window Flex one Piece
1	3571 112-3	MOULDING Vinyl Roof Trim Rear Side
1	3571 116-7	ANGLE SUPPORT Rear Window Upper Corner
1	3571 118	ANGLE SUPPORT Rear Window Upper
1	3571 119	REINFORCEMENT Rear Window Upper
1	3571 121	REAR WINDOW Glass Clear
14	3571 123	J-NUT Rod Grille Att. P & T Frame
1	3571 126-7	RETAINER Rear/Window H/Lining Side
1	3571 134-5	REINF. PLATE WING Vert-Stabilizer
2	3571 136	INSULATOR Vertical Stabilizer
1	3571 141	HOOD
2	3571 144	VERTICAL FIN Support Angle Bracket
2	3571 145	PIN STABILIZER Angle Limiting
1	3571 149	YOKE Extension Plate
2	3571 153	HEAD LAMP Hsg. Pivot Bracket
1	3571 165	PANEL Roof Ext.
1	3571 169	WIRING Bulkhead to Rad. Yoke
1	3571 181	PANEL Bulkhead Upper Closure
1	3571 182-3	RETAINER, Rear H/Lining Upper
1	3571 185	OIL COOLER Mtg. Bracket Hemi Eng. Only
1	3571 188	BRACKET Jack Towage
1	3571 194-5	MOULDING Qtr. o/Side Belt
2	3571 196	DECK LID Hinge Stop Bracket
4	3571 199	SPACER Park and Turn Signal Mounting
1	3571 202-3	TAPE Fender o/Side Color Dust Swirl
1	3571 197	WELD BOLT Jack Hold Down
1	2889 965	H/Lamp. Vac TANK BRKT. and VALVE
1	3412 766-7	H/LAMP housing Compartment (Partial)
1	3004 113	H/LAMP SWITCH
1	2864 029	H/LAMP Door actuator Switch
1	3403 092-3	LAMP, Park and Turn Signal
1	3784 EX9	R/WINDOW I/SIDE Mldg. Trim Joint Cap

From the racetrack to the street, Plymouth Superbirds left a legacy of performance. Here is a street version dressed up in pace car garb for the reunion at Atlanta Motor Speedway in 2016.